"PROTECTION FROM THE COLD"

COLD WAR PROTECTION IN PREPAREDNESS FOR NUCLEAR WAR

SIMON CRAINE
South Yorkshire Royal Observer Corps Museum

&

NOEL RYAN
Airfield Information Exchange & Airfield Research Group

© SY ROC Museum 2010

First Published 2011
Wildtrack Publishing

ISBN 978-1-904098-19-5

PHOTO, TEXT AND DRAWINGS COPYRIGHT:

All text unless otherwise specified is the copyright of the authors.

Photo copyright is held with the AiX Group except where secondary sources have been used. All secondary images are used with the permission of the original creator and have been sourced in the rear of the book.

In respect to sources; tracing of the original owner has been undertaken wherever possible, however where this has not been achieved then this will be highlighted in the photo list and the authors provide their apologies.

All drawings have been created through freehand electronic DTP software and are freehand representations of the original or secondary sources. This has involved no electronic transfer or storage of the source drawings / plans.

All mapping i.e. road network, EU boundaries is copyright of ESRI™.

CONTENTS

	PAGE
FOREWORD	7
PREFACE: Nuclear Infrastructure	11
SECTION 1: Nuclear Developments	16
Chapter 1: Introduction	17
SECTION 2: "The Need for Protection"	30
Chapter 2: Regional (Decentralised) Government	32
Chapter 3: Local Government	59
SECTION 3: Assisting Government	62
Chapter 4: Royal Observer Corps	63
Chapter 5: Civil / Home Defence	110
Chapter 6: Emergency Services	124
Chapter 7: Utilities	132
SECTION 4: Infrastructure Survey	143
Chapter 8: Regional / Local Authority Sites	144
Chapter 9: Royal Observer Corps Structures	165
Chapter 10: Utility Organisation Controlled Sites	220
SECTION 5: Further Research	234
INDEX	247

GEOFF CAMERON
1937 - 2005

This book is dedicated to Geoff Cameron whose humour and ideas have been inspirational and so he will never be forgotten for all the work that he did to bring together many people with a common interest.

FOREWORD

Background

This book was originally conceived to provide a comprehensive survey of the numerous underground nuclear Monitoring Posts in and around South Yorkshire during the period known as the "Cold War" (1946 to 1991). These sites were operated by the voluntary body of men and women of the Royal Observer Corps; whose origins date prior to World War 2 (WW2), and who occupied these Posts to provide a secretive warning and monitoring role in the event of a nuclear attack on the United Kingdom during the "Cold War". As the initial research to this book progressed; other protected sites were identified and were considered to be just as significant to the "Cold War" period and ultimately required inclusion.

Over the past years there have been extensive surveys of these sites which have been brought to the public's attention through the internet by organisations such as Subterranea Britannica (Sub-Brit) (http://www.subbrit.org.uk/) or through internet forum sites such as "28 Days Later" (http://www.28dayslater.co.uk/forums/). This book has never been intended to replicate the work already undertaken by these internet sites or indeed work already published by many other people's excellent books (see below).

Instead it aimed to complement such work by;

- providing a locally based context with respect to South Yorkshire;
- to enhance the understanding of the operational links between the numerous organisations operating such sites, and
- to identify the developmental changes to such organisations and sites during the period known as "The Cold War"

Sites relating to the organisations of the armed forces i.e. Army, Navy and Royal Air Force have purposefully been excluded from this work (except for brief mention) as jointly they could form a publication on their own, and to some degree, in this "day-and-age" be difficult to research considering present security implications.

The structure of the book was planned to be simplistic and not technical but to assist the lay person to understand the basics of the subject area and to progress their own research using the wealth of the other material produced by other organisations and groups. The rear of the book contains a list of key museums where people may visit to learn more about the subject area and the authors pay tribute to the excellent work undertaken by such organisations and the many other researchers covering the subject area over the years.

Key Work & Publications

Royal Observer Corps

In respect to the Royal Observer Corps praise has to be made to Derek Wood and his book "Attack Warning Red" which forms an incredible in-depth and concise history of the ROC. This book is essential reading for anyone interested in the ROC throughout its operational period from formation to stand-down. At a more local level, but just as concise, is the book by Charles Parker who in 1991 produced a concise history of the Corps entitled "The Royal Observer Corps in Lincolnshire 1936-1991".

This book although focusing on the Lincolnshire area from 1936, also includes a good historical introduction of the predecessors to the ROC of the Beacon Lighters from the reign of Edward II (1307 – 1327) and later during the threat from the Spanish Armada (1588) during the reign of Elizabeth I (1558 – 1603).

"Civil Protection / Defence"

"War Plan UK" was first published by Duncan Campbell in 1982 (2nd updated edition – 1983) and is generally seen as the ultimate source for the history and development of "Civil Defence" in the UK during the "Cold War". This book is equally complemented by "Beneath the City Streets" by Peter Laurie in 1979, which is generally seen as the book which brought many of the underground facilities to light and which focuses on many underground and protected government / military sites within the United Kingdom.

More recently has been the work undertaken by Sub-Brit (as discussed above) and especially the superb electronic publication linked to the Sub-Brit website by Steve Fox called "Struggle for Survival – Governing Britain after the Bomb" which has provided a modern day assessment of Cold War sites and structures above and below ground. In both cases, this work is well researched and worth viewing and most definitely complements the work by Campbell and Laurie. A further website is the forum based site "28 Days Later" (see above) which has further helped to progress interest on the subject through the internet.

More recent work undertaken by English Heritage culminated in 2004 with the excellent book *"The Cold War – Building for Nuclear Confrontation 1946 – 1989"*. The book covers a considerable in-depth survey of cold war buildings, airfields, nuclear weapons stores and bunkers and is backed up by excellent references and diagrams and is recommended reading for those interested in this period.

Research for this book has been difficult with many a dead-end and often no answer to enquiries. Considering that the purpose of this work is to enhance the educational potential of the subject area this is quite disappointing; however considering the generally secretive nature of the subject this may be partially justified. The subject area may be seen to be fluid. New information and buildings are forever being identified and praise has to be given to the many websites such as 28 Days Later and Sub-Brit which help to bring potential sites into the public realm.

Many sites may be restricted or are dangerous. The author therefore does not promote any unlawful trespass onto these properties without the proper permissions first being made from the landowner or organisation owning the property.

Assistance provided in the production of this book

Many have been willing to spend a little of their time to assist with information, contacts and sources, and the authors would like to thank the following people for which this work could not have been achieved.

- Noel Ryan of the Airfield Information Exchange (AIX) and Airfield Research Group (ARG) for the support offered in the photographing of numerous Cold War related sites.
- John Shere for his valuable insight into the Cold War and extensive knowledge and experience of missile systems.
- Edwina Holden and Lawrence Holmes of the Royal Observer Corps Association (ROCA) whose help in searching out sources and contacts and especially knowledge and friendship has been so welcome.
- Neville Cullingford of the Royal Observer Corps Museum Trust for the help in locating pictures of ROC sites.
- Charles Parker and Peter Jex of the Lincoln 15 Group ROCA branch for their help and assistance in sourcing images of the ROC Group Control at Fiskerton Nr Lincoln.
- Chris Howells; for the permission to use his excellent pictures of the restored ROC 20 Group Control building in York.
- Mark Johnson for the supply of a number of images relating to the ROC and AFS; for pulling together informative text on the AFS and for the many hours of enjoyment in his small but quite agile aircraft.
- English Heritage at Swindon for their permission to utilise their excellent "Cold War" publication in the development of a number of the building plans.
- Zvi Golod and Todd Miller of Satellite Mediaport Services Ltd at the Lawford Heath Earth Station for their help and assistance in the acquisition of pictures regarding the former ROC Lawford Heath Group Control site.
- The many other people and organisations that have assisted in this work, and who are too many to name but are gratefully thanked.

PREFACE

NUCLEAR INFRASTRUCTURE

The words *"Nuclear Bunkers"* generate images of vast reinforced concrete structures buried deep underground. The sanctuary of the chosen few following a nuclear attack on the country – Royalty, key Government figures, top military personnel and perhaps leaders of industry. Certainly such structures did exist for that very purpose; the continuity of administration after a nuclear attack was a prime concern, but what would be left to govern after the attack was another matter. Less well known is that during the Cold War, a huge network of protected structures existed. These were relics from WW2 or were new purpose built structures. These ranged from;

- Anti Aircraft Operations Rooms (AAOR);
- Civil Defence Corps Operations Rooms;
- Borough and Local Authority Controls;
- Sector and Group Controls to over 1500 three-person underground Monitoring Posts operated by the Royal Observer Corps;
- Regional Government HQs;
- Home Defence forces including Nuclear Reporting Cells (NRC); and,
- Utility Organisation Sites including Water, Electricity and Telecommunications.

For most of the Cold War period (1946 – 1991); following a nuclear attack, the United Kingdom Warning and Monitoring Organisation (UKWMO) would be responsible for the plotting and recording of nuclear bursts and resultant radioactive fallout. A complex organisation; the UKWMO in simplistic terms: **collected**, **collated** and **interpreted** information from the nationwide Royal Observer Corps Monitoring Posts and other reporting sources. The predicted path of fallout was then made available to the authorities of the areas concerned. They in turn would issue the relevant warnings.

The ability to govern centrally would not have been possible, at least initially. The plan was that the country would be governed by a strategic chain of command; initially by Regional Commissioners from already established "Regional Seats of Government" (RSG) through to local authorities, operating from Borough controls. The organisation required to govern locally was complex, and probably unworkable had the worst happened.

The cornerstone of the "Cold" War not turning "Hot" was the appropriate acronym "MAD." which stood for "Mutually Assured Destruction". The MAD doctrine ensured that World peace was maintained by the fact that once Warsaw Pact missiles and bombers were detected as "incoming", NATO's missiles and aircraft would be in the air to provide a retaliatory strike – in reality; to start a war would lead to certain self destruction.

During a speech by Queen Elizabeth II in 1980 it was said:

"Their awesome destructive power has preserved the world from major war for the past 35 years. So far nuclear weapons have served as a deterrent. But for the bomb to remain a threat, politicians must be seen to be prepared to use it. There are no winners in the nuclear arms race. What happened at Hiroshima should serve to remind the world of the nightmarish consequences of nuclear war. If the memory of that city's suffering will prevent a future Armageddon, then the children of Hiroshima will have not died in vain"

Structure of this Book

The following chapters provide a survey of the infrastructure utilised by many of the civil protection organisations that existed during the Cold War. The book generally focuses on examples taken from within the South Yorkshire County Area or its surrounding environs. These structures will form those which would have provided a "protective" capability for a number of "official" organisations and their staff, to undertake significant roles in the period before, during and after a nuclear attack on the United Kingdom.

The initial time period which this book will concentrate, will be the period commonly known as the "Cold War". Although there has been debate on the actual start of the "Cold War"; for this book this period will range from 1946 to 1991.

1946 forms the year of the initial increase in tensions between the USSR and US / UK and is the year when the "Iron Curtain" was first mentioned in a speech by former Prime Minister Winston Churchill which stated; while **1991** forms the year of the failure of a communist-led coup d'état against Mikhail Gorbachev in the Soviet Union in August 1991 and which contributed towards the ending of the communist party's control of the military and government and ultimate Soviet Union dissolution on 25th December 1991.

Section 1: provides the reader with an insight into the "Cold War". It provides a comprehensive overview which provides context into the physical actions of the time, the powers at work and complexities which led to the need for key operational organisations and infrastructures.

Section 2: provides the reader with an insight into the need for such infrastructure. The section focuses on the role of both central and local government and their overall objectives and needs for protected accommodation.

Section 3: identifies the operational organisations that would have provided assistance to central and local governments, in the maintenance of control, law and order or provision of resources.

The section therefore describes these organisations' roles and operations during the "conflict" period. Organisations which will be included and hence will play a large part within this history include;

- Civil Defence Corps
- Royal Observer Corps
- Utility Organisations

Section 4: will then aim to provide a survey of such protected sites which existed or still exist within the South Yorkshire County or in some cases exist(ed) outside the county but had significant influence upon the operations within.

Section 5: provides the basis for further research for those wishing to learn more about the subject. The sources are not exhaustive but aim to provide a balanced coverage of the subject area and a good starting point for study.

Points to Note

1.　This book has utilised a number of key sources to expand the context of this work. Such sources have been referenced where used and included as a list in the rear of the book. In all cases this list provides an effective source for further research and to provide greater insight into areas covered within the text.

2.　The book refers to the County of South Yorkshire as the main Metropolitan area consisting of the four districts of Sheffield, Rotherham, Barnsley and Doncaster. This area was created as a result of the Local Government Act 1972 and therefore was not in existence during the initial stages of the "cold war" period. For clarity and consistency, this area will be referred to throughout the full time period of the organisations being studied including those periods before the county's inception.

3.　The policies and key objectives developed in respect to a potential nuclear attack are based upon a systematic approach relating to the time periods leading towards and after the potential attack. These periods are;

- Pre-Attack (Dispersion & Sheltering) – 2 Weeks
- Attack – 1 Day
- Post Attack (Fallout) – 2 Weeks
- Recovery (Collection & integration of human & physical assets) – 6 Months
- Long Term Recovery – 2 to 5 Years
- Long Term Medical & Genetic Effects – 20 to 50 Years

4.　In the research of sites, the authors have aimed to respect the wishes of the owners of the cold war sites. In some cases this has involved the limiting of information used in this book.

SECTION 1

"NUCLEAR" DEVELOPMENTS

CHAPTER 1
INTRODUCTION

A Nuclear World Begins

The world's first nuclear weapons were developed by the US at the Los Alamos range and dropped on the Japanese cities of Hiroshima and Nagasaki on the 6th and 9th August 1945 respectively. The scientist, J Robert Oppenheimer, a key figure in the development of these weapons, on the 16th October 1945, said:

"If atomic bombs are to be added to the arsenals of a warring world then the time will come when mankind will curse the name of Los Alamos & Hiroshima. The peoples of the world must unite or they will surely perish"

The first atomic weapon to be used in anger – "Little Boy"

Hiroshima after the bomb

"Cold War"

Almost from the end of WW2, tensions between the East and West were building up as the US, UK and Soviet Union was trying to gain the greatest benefit from the defeated Germany. In a speech by Stalin in February 1946, grave concerns were raised in the West as Stalin's speech undertook a strong Marxist-Leninist line signifying that capitalism made war inevitable;

"The development of world capitalism proceeds not in the path of smooth and even progress but through crisis and the catastrophes of war".

Winston Churchill, who had been ousted from office by Clement Atlee in the 1945 general election, responded to this statement in an address to the Westminster College at Fulton, Missouri in March 1946.

"From Stettin in the Baltic to Trieste in the Adriatic, an iron curtain has descended across the continent"

American public opinion saw the speech to be too extreme and which was denounced by most of the press. In Moscow it was seen by Stalin as confirming his suspicions of the West's hostility towards the Soviet Union.

Nuclear Tensions

Although the main tensions grew out of actions on the European front especially centred on Germany, a number of other areas of the world saw significant tensions between supporters of the capitalist based principles of the "West" and those supporting the communist policies of the "East". Significant conflicts include;

- The Soviet blockade of Berlin (1948 – 1949) as a result of proposed currency reforms in the Western sectors of Berlin.
- The invasion of South Korea by North Korea (1949 – 1953)
- The US (CIA) orchestrated Guatemalan coup d'état (1954)
- War between North and South Vietnam (1954 – 1975)
- The Suez Crisis (1956)
- The quashing of the Hungarian uprising by the Soviet Union (1956)
- Further tensions in Berlin and subsequent building of the Berlin Wall (1958 – 1961)
- Cuban Missile Crisis when the Soviet Union threatened to locate nuclear weapons in Cuba and right on the doorstep of the United States (1962)
- The invasion of Prague by Soviet troops to halt political reforms (1968)
- The invasion of Afghanistan by Soviet troops (1979)

Of the above, the following are deemed to offer significant key points in the rise of nuclear tension between the Russia and US / UK.

Berlin Blockade (1948)

Following the end of the Second World War; Germany had been divided between America, Great Britain, Russia and France. Within the Russian zone, which comprised much of eastern

Germany, was the City of Berlin which had been further divided between the allies into similar respective sectors. The basis of an economically-stable Western Germany was seen by the Western allies as being achievable through the reform of the unstable 'Reichsmark' German currency introduced after the war and which had gradually devalued through excessive printing leading to over circulation.

In February 1948, the Americans and British proposed to the Allied Control Council that a new German currency should be created. The Soviets opposed such reforms and refused to accept the proposal on the basis that strengthening the German economy would undermine their policy of ensuring a weak Germany. Anticipating the introduction of a new currency by the other countries in the non-Soviet zones, in May 1948, the Soviet Union directed its military to introduce its own new currency and to permit only the Soviet currency to be used in their occupied Berlin area.

On 18th June 1948, the United States, Britain and France announced that, on 21st June, the 'Deutschmark' would be used much to the annoyance of the Soviets who refused to permit its use as legal tender in Berlin. The following day, the Soviet Union started to close the borders of their sector of Germany, and eventually by the 25th June, they had cut all roads, rail and water access into the Western Region of Berlin (located within the Soviet controlled East Germany) thereby isolating the allied sectors of the city. The only means of getting the food, water, coal and other materials needed for survival was by air. So began the biggest operation of air supply in history, *The Berlin Airlift*.

Utilising three main air corridors over East German territory into Berlin's Templehof and Gatow airports, the western allies made over 278,000 flights over the 15 months of the blockade and carried over 2.3 million tons of cargo. The continued success of the Airlift by the allied forces was seen to humiliate the Soviets who realised that they were losing the propaganda war. Reporting on the 15 April 1949, the Soviet news agency *TASS* reported that the Soviet Union would be willing to lift the blockade. Soon after, the four powers began serious negotiations, and a settlement was made on Allied terms. Finally on 4th May 1949, the Allies announced that an agreement to end the blockade, in eight days, had been reached.

The Soviet blockade of Berlin was lifted at one minute after midnight, on 12th May 1949 and a British convoy immediately drove through to Berlin, with the first train from West Germany reaching Berlin at 05:32. The airlift continued for a further four months in order to amass enough reserves and the allies were confident that the blockade would not be re-imposed The blockade officially ending on 30th September 1949.

Country	No of Flights	%	Tons of Cargo	%
United Kingdom	87,841	31.57	541,937	23.30
United States	189,963	68.28	1,783,573	76.67
France	424	0.15	896	0.03
TOTAL	**278,228**	**100**	**2,326,406**	**100**

Source: Truman Library [Online]

Berlin Airlift Statistics
(26th June 1948 to 30th Sept 1949)

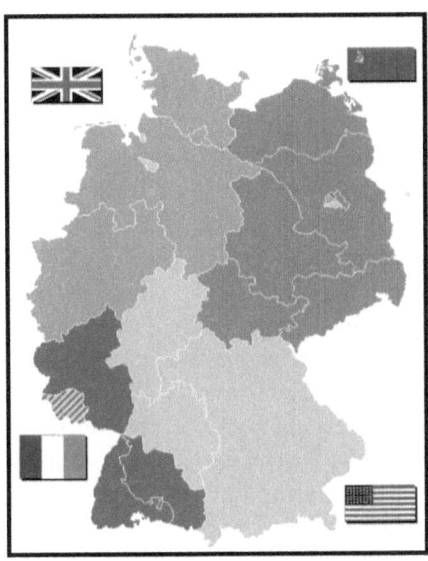

The division of Germany amongst the allies
Source: Wikipedia

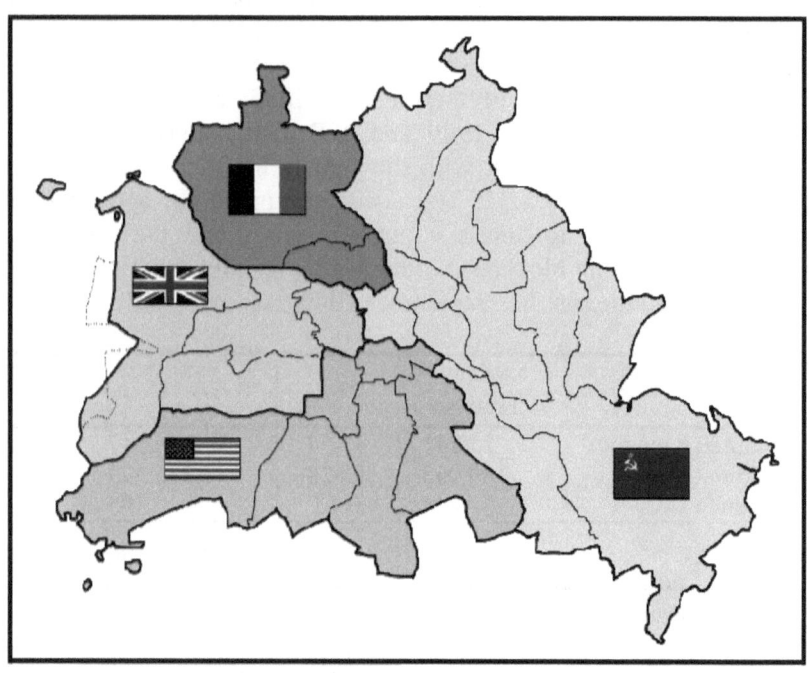

The division of Berlin amongst the allies
Source: Wikipedia

Construction of the Berlin Wall (1961)

After 1945, the three zones of occupation in West Germany and the Soviet occupied zone grew apart both politically and economically. The creation of the two states in 1949; the German Federal Republic (*Bundesrepublik Deutschland*) and German Democratic Republic (*Deutsche Demokratische Republik*) led to the strengthening of this split; with the Federal Republic (West Germany) focusing upon economic and political principles of the West and the Democratic Republic (East Germany) focusing on Soviet Communist principles. As a result of this Soviet Communist ideology in which the East German governmental principles were entwined, many East German people fled to the West to escape the political and social pressure and domination of all spheres of life by the state and Communist led party that prevailed.

Between 1949 and 1960 the exodus of people was averaging 300,000 per annum and hence by 1960, the combination of the effects of World War II and the massive emigration westward, left East Germany with only 61% of its population of working age, compared to 70.5% before the war. The loss was disproportionately heavy amongst professionals such as teachers, engineers, technicians, doctors, lawyers and skilled workers.

The ruling East German communist party (*Sozialistische Einheitspartei Deutschlands* – SED) were worried about the haemorrhaging of the country's skills and resources as a result. Sealing off all borders between East and West was seen by the East German regime to be the only available course of action to stop the exodus and prevent a resultant collapse of the East German Economy.

Construction of the Wall

Although defiantly stating on the 15th June 1961, that "no-one has any intention of building a wall"; on the 12th August 1961, Walter Ulbricht, the First Secretary of the Socialist Unity Party and GDR State Council chairman signed an agreement with Soviet Premier Nikita Khrushchev to close the border and erect a wall. In the early hours of 13th August 1961, the closure of all routes out of the Soviet sector into West Berlin began with the laying of barbed wire. Within a few days, the barbed wire fences laid on the 13th August were replaced with more substantial barricades forming a brick and barbed wire built wall. Through the years, the Berlin Wall evolved through four versions:

1. Barbed wire fence (1961)
2. Improved brick and wire fence (1961/2 –1965)
3. Concrete panelled wall (1965–1975)
4. Grenzmauer 75 / Border Wall 75 consisting of 'L' shaped concrete panels with concrete tube 'anti-grab' tube along the top (1975–1989)

The final generation of the wall from 1975 is the construction which is synonymous as the Berlin Wall. It consisted of separate sections of reinforced concrete, and each being 3.6 metres (12 ft) high and 1.2 metres (3.9 ft) wide. The top of the wall was lined with a smooth pipe, intended to make it more difficult to scale.

Though the wall was designated by the regime as an "anti-fascist" wall, its purpose was to stem the exodus to the West of East German citizens. Regulations issued by the East German Government also led to citizens in the East of Berlin and East Germany, no longer being able to travel into West Berlin. West Berlin was ultimately sealed off by the wall and the mass exodus of citizens from East to West Berlin significantly reduced. The regulations also applied to the 65,000 East Berlin residents who commuted and studied daily in West Berlin. By 1961 approximately three million people had left East Germany for the West. Most were reluctant to leave, but economic and social conditions in the East drove them away.

The closing of the barriers and subsequent building of the wall ultimately served its purpose. The constant flow of migrants into West Berlin was considerably reduced to a trickle from the 300,000 per annum between 1949 and 1961 to 22,000 per annum after 1962. (see graph below).

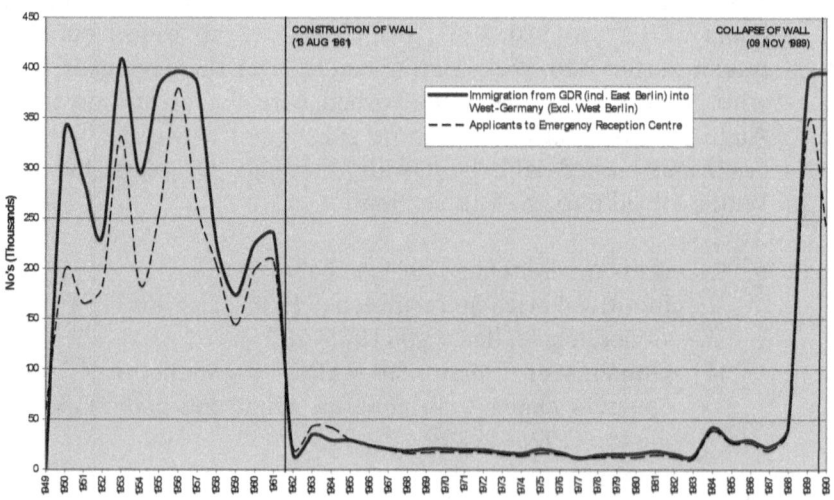

Immigration from East to West Germany and comparison of respective applications at Emergency Reception Centres
Source: Marienfelde Refugee Centre Museum

Berlin Stand-off: Confrontation at the Wall (1961)

During the Potsdam Conference at the end of WW2, an agreement had been made to allow Allied personnel free access in any sector of Berlin without any passport checks by East German police. This therefore allowed members of the Allied Forces, foreigners and diplomats free access to enter East Berlin at the Friedrichstraße border crossing ("Checkpoint Charlie") without any checks or delay. With the building of the Berlin Wall in August 1961 and closure of many of the former crossing points between east and west, the Friedrichstraße border crossing formed the main crossing point for access into East Berlin.

On the 22nd October 1961, East German border guards tried to undertake checks on the US Chief of Mission in West Berlin as he attempted to enter East German at Checkpoint Charlie in order to visit the Theatre in East Berlin. Apart from going against the Potsdam Agreement it was seen by the US as undermining the rights not just of the US personnel but also those of the allies in Berlin as a whole.

In order to "test-the-water" US General Lucius D. Clay sent an American diplomat in a clearly recognisable diplomatic vehicle, to try to access through into East Berlin at the checkpoint. The diplomat was duly stopped by East German transport police who asked to see his passport. Once his identity had been identified, US Military Police were sent in to enable the diplomatic car to be escorted through into East Germany unhindered. Shocked East German police got out of the way and allowed access for the diplomatic vehicle. The car continued and the soldiers returned to West Berlin. A further British diplomat was stopped the following day which infuriated General Clay further who instigated the use of US Jeeps to convoy US civilians into East Berlin over the next few days.

The repeated Soviet-instigated efforts to restrict access by American personnel to the Soviet sector continued and substantially increased tensions in Berlin and resulting in considerable resentment within the US and Allied Forces. The American leadership; General Clay, acting in Berlin as the envoy of President John F. Kennedy; the U.S. Commander in Berlin, Major General Albert Watson; and Diplomat Allan Lightner, Jr., the senior State Department representative, were determined to ensure access across borders was unrestricted as previously agreed at Potsdam in 1945, while at the same time stressing the point that they would not recognize the East German border guards as having any authority in Berlin. To signal American and Allied determination to maintain access rights, the U.S. Army moved ten M-48A1 tanks and three M-59 armoured personnel carriers to Checkpoint Charlie.

On the morning of the 27th October thirty-three Soviet tanks were deployed to the Brandenburg Gate with ten continuing onto the Friedrichstraße border crossing and halting within 100m of the US armoury. The attention of the world was now fixed on Berlin. American and Soviet tanks, barely one hundred metres apart, faced each other for approximately sixteen hours with their main guns trained on each other. At the same time, American military and diplomatic personnel with military police escorts continued to move through the checkpoint, exercising their rights to travel into the Soviet sector.

Kennedy, not wishing to escalate the situation held secret talks with an aim to solve the situation. With the Soviet Secret Police (KGB) listening in, Soviet President Nikita Khrushchev was well aware of the planning of this meeting. He was adamant that all the American Generals wanted, was to test, and had indeed tested, the resolve of the Soviet Generals.

Eventually as a result of an agreement between Kennedy and Khrushchev, the following day, Soviet tanks were withdrawn to a fallback position; being closely followed by the US. Both countries saw themselves as victors of the situation. The Soviets were hailed as heroes over their stance in the situation however US General Clay's objective was also achieved. His aim was to get the Soviets to the border and show to the world that the government in East Germany was a 'puppet regime' with East Germany being a satellite state of the Soviet Union who was ultimately in charge; this General Clay succeeded in doing.

Cuban Missile Crisis (1962)

The Cuban Missile Crisis is seen as the nearest the world came to nuclear war during this period. The United States was at its highest ever state of readiness and Soviet field commanders in Cuba were apparently prepared to use battlefield nuclear weapons to defend the island if it was invaded.

Castro comes to power

Since 1898 the United States had played a major role in liberating Cuba of Spanish colonial oppression and ultimately to protect considerable American investment. By the 1950's however; the incumbent Cuban leader Fulgencio Batista y Zaldivar who came to power in 1933 was losing considerable support through his developed corrupt and dictatorial regime. On the 25th July 1953 a young lawyer called Fidel Castro first raised the standard of a revolution towards Batista. As a result Castro was captured and imprisoned. Having being released into exile in Mexico, Castro returned to Cuba to fight a two year guerrilla struggle to overthrow Batista.

In 1959 he was successful and formed a new coalition government in Cuba. The government followed a Cuban Nationalist policy which ultimately led to the nationalisation of much of the American interests within Cuba. Such a move led to US reprisals in the form of economic blockade of the country and ultimately Castro looked towards the Soviet Union for support. The failed "Bay of Pigs" invasion in 1961 when the US backed Cuban exiles attempted to overthrow the socialist government of Cuba; the Fidel Castro, felt that a second attack was almost inevitable.

Defending the island however was not going to be easy, given the vast resources that the US had to launch an invasion. In 1962 Castro looked towards Soviet Premier Khrushchev to assist Castro in defending Cuba and which ultimately led to the locating of strategic nuclear missiles on the island. By 1962, the Soviet Union was behind the United States in the arms race. Soviet missiles were only powerful enough to be launched against Europe but U.S. missiles were capable of striking anywhere in the Soviet Union. In late April 1962, Khrushchev conceived the idea of placing intermediate-range missiles in Cuba; a Soviet allied country lying at its closest approximately 100 miles from the US mainland (Florida) and approximately 1200 miles from the US Capital (Washington DC). Such a deployment was seen to double the Soviet strategic arsenal and provide a real deterrent to a potential U.S. attack against the Soviet Union.

The "crisis" for the US began on 15th October 1962 when reconnaissance photographs taken over Cuba, revealed Soviet missiles under construction in Cuba. The thought of "Soviet" nuclear weapons being so close to the US mainland caused grave concern for US President Kennedy who was informed about the installations early the next day. At once President Kennedy organized the Executive Committee of the United States National Security Council (EX-COMM), a group of his twelve most important advisors to handle the crisis to discuss the situation and progress reaction to the threat.

After seven days of guarded and intense debate within the upper echelons of government, Kennedy concluded to impose a naval quarantine around Cuba. He wished to prevent the arrival of more Soviet offensive weapons on the island. On 22nd October 1962, Kennedy announced the discovery of the missile installations to the public and his decision to quarantine the island. He proclaimed that any nuclear missile launched from Cuba would "… be regarded as an attack on the United States by the Soviet Union" and demanded that "… the Soviets remove all their offensive weapons from Cuba". As a result of this communiqué, tensions began to build on both sides. Kennedy ordered low-level reconnaissance missions once every two hours in order to monitor the situation both on land and sea and by the 25th October; Kennedy had pulled the quarantine line back and raised military readiness to DEFCON 2 [1].

---

[1] DEFCON (DEFense readiness CONdition) is a measure of the activation and readiness level of the United States Armed Forces. Standard peacetime protocol is DEFCON 5, and increasing through to DEFCON 1 which represents expectation of actual imminent attack. The UK equivalent is referred to as the BIKINI STATE.

On the 26th October; the US National Security Council received a letter from Khrushchev in which he proposed removing Soviet missiles and personnel from Cuba; however this would only be undertaken if the United States would guarantee not to invade. This "ray-of-light" was however short-lived, as the next day a U-2 spy-plane was shot down over Cuba and the US Security Council received a second letter from Khrushchev with further demands as a result; the removal of U.S. missiles in Turkey in exchange for Soviet missiles in Cuba. Attorney General Robert Kennedy suggested ignoring the second letter and contacted Soviet Ambassador Anatoly Dobrynin to tell him of the U.S. agreement with the first.

Tensions finally eased on the 28th October; when Khrushchev announced that he would dismantle the installations and return the missiles to the Soviet Union, expressing his trust that the United States would not invade Cuba. Further negotiations were held to implement the October 28th agreement, including a United States demand that Soviet light bombers be removed from Cuba, and specifying the exact form and conditions of United States assurances not to invade Cuba.

SECTION 2
"THE NEED FOR PROTECTION"

MAINTAINING GOVERNMENT & SOCIAL SERVICES

TO RECAP ...

The previous section highlighted the initial key tensions that existed during the early period of the Cold War between the East and West.

It has to be stressed that the cold war period was not just limited to these tensions but relations between the East and West varied "for better or worse" over its period until the final thaw within the 1990s. Other accounts suggest that there may have been two main Cold War periods where tensions were at their highest; during the 1960s as highlighted above and during the late 1970s. During both these periods, nuclear war was seen as a definite possibility and the ability for the country to survive such an attack was seen as being dependent on effective management of the country, through its people and resources.

Protected accommodation was essential to maintain a satisfactory level of control, prior to or during an attack and to reconstruct the country afterwards. Such sites had to be effective and built to provide a level of protection capable preventing annihilation during the attack period. As the power of nuclear weapons increased, then the ability for those protected sites to be able to withstand the forces generated by such weapons also increased, necessitating either a redevelopment of existing sites or development of new sites to maintain an effective protective capability.

What has to be remembered is that Central Government planning and policy making throughout this period (and during times of relative "peace") was (and still is) fluid. Changes in Government leadership; developments in new technology, budgetary constraints and economic conditions all impact upon the development of an effective policy to minimise the risk of annihilation enabling the country to recover if the worst happened. The following chapter therefore focuses on these changing requirements in order to maintain Governmental control before, during and after a potential nuclear attack at both national (central) and local levels and therefore the chapter provides the reader with a brief understanding of the Regional and Local Government structures that developed throughout the period; how these were structured and controlled and provide a base for further research.

CHAPTER 2

REGIONAL (DECENTRALISED) GOVERNMENT

The Need for Protection: Radiation & Fallout – "The Science Bit"

If nuclear weapons are used on a large scale, those of us living in the country areas might be exposed to as great a risk as those in the towns. Following a nuclear bomb-burst apart from the high intensity blast and heat effects which account for approximately 45% and 35% of the energy from the explosion respectively; a high amount of radiation is also emitted. This radiation consists of two kinds.

1. **Initial nuclear radiation:** This is radiation emitted within the first minute after detonation and results almost entirely from the nuclear processes occurring at detonation. This accounts for 5% of the energy released from the explosion.
2. **Residual radiation:** This is radiation which is emitted later than 1 minute after detonation and arises principally from the decay of radio-isotopes produced during the explosion. This accounts for 15% of the energy released from the explosion.

The effects of the detonation of a nuclear device will vary considerably depending upon the height of the explosion and may consist of;

1. **Ground Burst:** This occurs when the nuclear explosion detonates at ground level or close to the ground so that the fireball touches the ground surface. In general terms, if an explosion occurs close to the ground, then dust and debris is sucked up into the atmosphere by the explosion and radiated by the explosion. After being dispersed by any subsequent wind, it falls across the country as radioactive particles, commonly known as fallout.

    The size of these particles will determine how far they will travel by the prevailing wind – The larger the particles then the less distance they will travel with the prevailing wind. The radioactive dust, falling where the wind blows it, will bring the most widespread dangers.

2. **Air Burst**[2]: This occurs when the resultant fireball explodes in the air and is clear of the ground surface. In this case little debris and dust particles are lifted into the sky and therefore the risk from radioactive fallout is significantly reduced when compared to ground burst. High altitude air bursts may be used to disrupt radio communications and damage items that contain electronic components through the effects of a generated Electro-magnetic Pulse (EMP).

3. **Water Burst:** These occur when the nuclear explosion detonates in shallow water or at such a height that the subsequent fireball generated by the explosion touches the water surface. In such cases large quantities of water and sediment (if shallow water) are lifted miles into the sky which is then deposited as rain which brings with it radioactive particles to the ground.

The risk of fallout therefore highlights the fact that no part of the United Kingdom could be considered safe from both the direct effects of the weapons (Heat and Blast) and the resultant fallout (Radiation).

---

[2] Also includes an explosion on the fringe of the earth's atmosphere

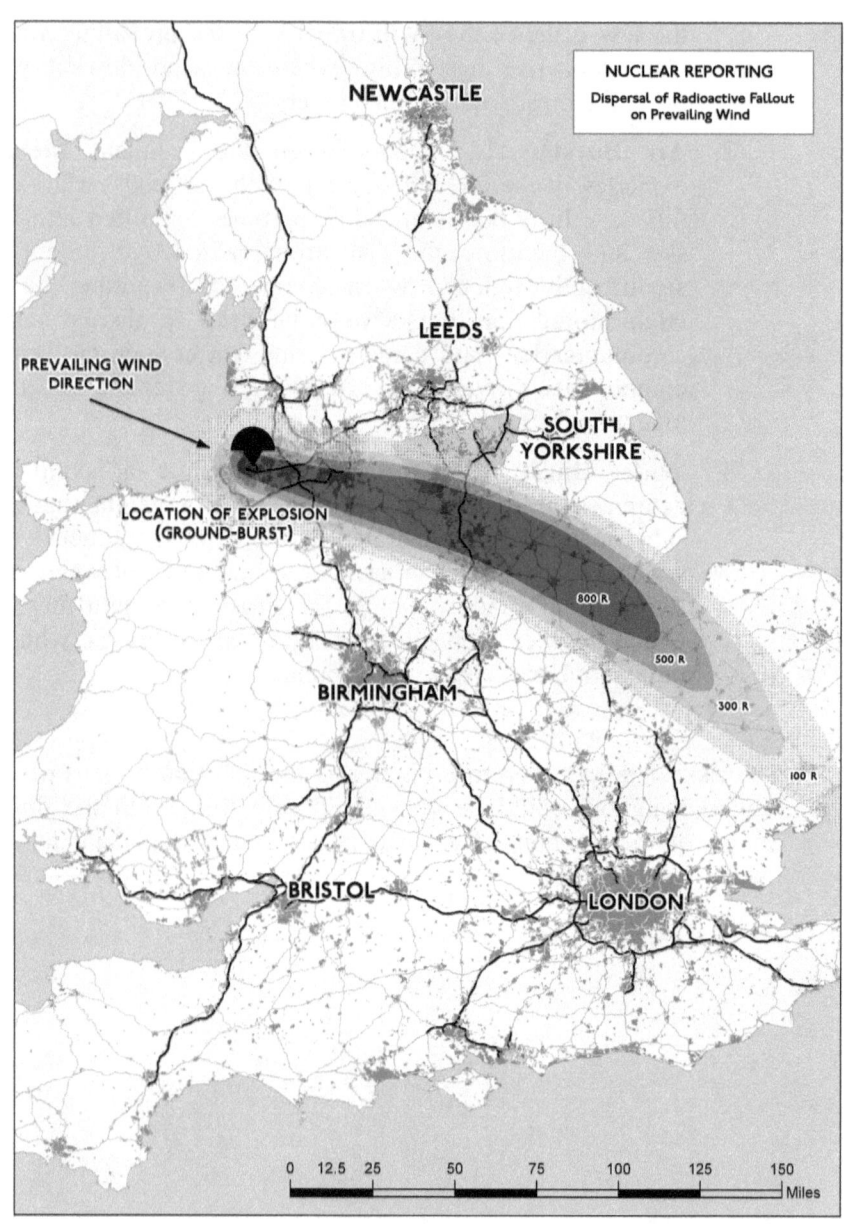

Example of the Dispersal of Nuclear Fallout on Prevailing Winds from a Ground Burst on Liverpool. The dispersal pattern of nuclear fallout is comparable with that of the volcanic ash cloud from the Icelandic Eyjafjallajökull volcano that erupted during 2010.
Source: SYROCM

Survivability

Survivability of the effects of radiation can be achieved by following the application of three factors.

1. **DISTANCE:** The greater the distance between the radiation source and the recipient then the less will be the overall radiation dose received.

2. **SHEILDING:** Depending upon the types of radiation source, certain materials may restrict or reduce the dose-rate reaching the potential recipient. Gamma rays as generated by a nuclear explosion have the ability to penetrate a wide variety of materials, however the more dense the material, then the greater the protection from radiation. For instance, in order to reduce the radiation dose-rate by half, a concrete barrier would need to be approximately 5 to 6 cm thick, while a barrier using earth would need to be 8 to 9cm thick. This protection afforded by these materials was referred to as the materials "Protection Factor".

3. **DECAY:** The level of radiation over time reduces by half its dose rate value over a set period of time. This time period; known as the radiation sources "half-life" depends on the source. A general rule of thumb is that as time increases by a factor of 7; then the intensity of the radiation falls by a factor of 10. Thus if the dose rate after 1 hour is 100CgY then after 7 hours the value is 10CgY; 49 hours (2 days) it is 1 CgY; 343 hours (2 weeks) it is 0.1CgY etc.

Based on these principles the ability of a building to protect occupants from radiation is related to its size, construction and location of occupants.

The booklet issued by the government in the 1950's called "Advising the Householder on the Effects of Nuclear Weapons" and later in the 1980's called "Protect and Survive"; stressed that in respect to residential buildings such as houses, any potential shelters should be located away from the outer walls of the building (preferably central) and that offered effective protection in the event of collapse. In terms of protected sites for the Government, and other organisations required to maintain essential services after a potential attack the protection offered by such buildings would need to be considerable, especially as such sites may be seen as potential targets.

The changes in nuclear weapons technology since the 1950s in respect to yield and power has therefore led to considerable reappraisal of the buildings used by such governments and organisations in order to maintain a suitable level of protection. This may generally be seen by the changes in buildings from War Rooms through to Sub Regional HQs etc; and partly offers the reasoning for greater protection being provided for sites on the East of the country (deemed to have a greater risk of attack) which are generally fully sunk sites than those on the West which are only partly sunk[3] (and deemed to be at less risk from attack).

Towards War

Since the late 1950s the Government and military have undertaken numerous exercises in order to anticipate the overall effect of an attack on the United Kingdom. These scenarios have generally focused on a systematic development of stages leading up to, during and after an attack in order to anticipate the potential requirement, resources and personnel required, to effectively govern the country throughout the period.

These stages and generally assumed but approximate time-scales include;

- Pre-Attack (Dispersion & Sheltering) – 2 Weeks
- Attack – 1 Day
- Post Attack (Fallout) – 2 Weeks
- Initial Recovery (Collection & integration of human & physical assets) – 6 Months

---

[3] This may be seen from the Museums at Kelvedon Hatch, Holmpton and Anstruther in the East of the country being fully protected underground sites and Hack Green in the West being partly protected semi-sunk.

- Long Term Recovery – 2 to 5 Years
- Long Term Medical & Genetic Effects – 20 to 50 Years

Government documents produced during the 1980s stated that Nuclear War without warning would not be thrust upon the population of the United Kingdom[4]. In effect, there would be a significant escalation of tensions which could ultimately lead to all-out attack with conventional and / or nuclear weapons. This time period is generally deemed to be approximately 2 weeks; however this period would possibly vary depending on the situation and very possibly could have been a matter of a day. The Government would generally delay the preparations for war and warnings to the public to the last minute in order to mitigate any potential absenteeism, and undue panic that the warnings would have on the public.

After the Attack

During the first few weeks after a nuclear attack, centralised and local authorities would be unable to provide any practical help or assistance to the population as a result of the disruption and breakdown of key services. The solution was therefore seen to lie with a de-centralisation of government control to a level which would have provided the best management and control of factors such as law and order, to preserve health and safeguard resources.

This idea was not new; but based on Home Defence regions created during WW2 which would have been headed by Regional Commissioners serving each region. Although during the Cold War there were a number of structural changes, the main body of a regionalised structure was still apparent. This structure, in the majority of cases, was assisted by sub-level organisations (i.e. Sub-Regional Controls) and these were linked to other strategic organisations within the region i.e. County and Borough Controls. These sub-level organisations generally operated from their own centres of control and controlled a smaller geographic and focused area but with communication links back to the regional organisations.

---

[4] Home Office Emergency Services Circular ES1/1981 et al

Between 1946 and 1991 there were a number of significant changes made to the planned regional structures. These formed the main body of regional control and consisted of;

- Regional War Rooms (1950s)
- Regional Seats of Government (1950s – 1970s)
- Sub-Regional Controls (1950s – 1970s)
- Sub-Regional HQs (1970s – 1980s)
- Regional Government HQs (1980s – 1990s)

In respect to the Regional Seats of Government and Sub Regional Controls, these organisations were interlinked during the early 1960s, however, gradually over time; greater emphasis was placed upon the Sub-Regional areas and the development of the controls to govern these smaller geographic areas.

Control Levels

Although there were a number of changes to regional government between 1948 and 1991; the main backbone of the system consisted of a systematic set of levels based on geographic coordination areas. These levels ranged from Regional through to Local level. There was no guarantee that the Regional Government Control system could function effectively from the time it was required and therefore this was only to offer the potential to support levels higher in the command structure if in the aftermath of a nuclear attack, control at the official level was lost for sometime. As a result, the control system would potentially have to be extended down to a parish or even to a lower community level (hamlet, village, ward or street) within the "local" area if required.

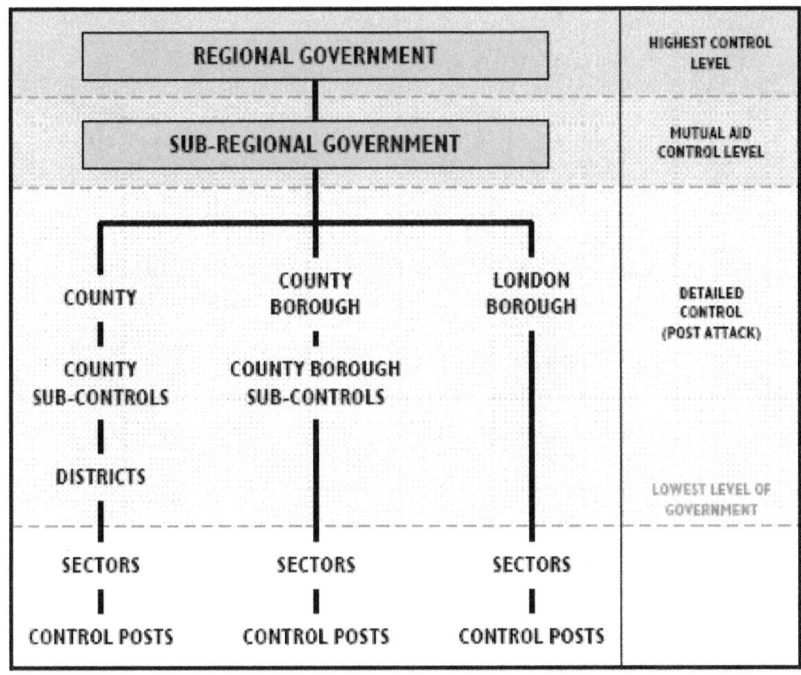

Control Chain Levels (c.1971)

The control system related to these levels varied also, however common roles may be identified;

LEVEL	STRUCTURE
Regional	Headed by a Regional Commissioner and assisted by a Deputy Regional Commissioner and a staff of civil servants, representatives of the Public Utilities, industry, Armed Forces, Police and Judiciary.
	The Regional Commissioner and his Deputy would each occupy a separate Zone Headquarters. This would enable the Regional Commissioner temporarily to delegate control of one Zone to Deputy, if necessary while he controlled the other.
	Both Zone headquarters would be staffed in a time of rising tension but would have no executive function until, as a result of attack, central government had ceased to function.
Sub-Regional	Headed by a Sub-Regional Commissioner, the commissioner and deputy would have the overall responsibility for the control of "civil defence" operations within the sub-region, including the deployment of mobile forces and organisation of reinforcement to counties and county boroughs requiring assistance after the attack, and ultimately to provide for a further decentralisation of the "central government" within each region". They would also have had a pivotal role between the policymaking Regional Government and the local authorities with their extended wartime functions.
County	Headed by a controller with a small advisory Emergency Committee of elected members and staffed by Local Authority officials and liaison representatives similar to those at Zone Headquarters.
District	Headed by a controller with a small advisory Emergency Committee of elected members and staffed by Local Authority officials with liaison officers from certain Government Departments, Public Utilities and Industry.

Regional War Rooms - RWR (1952 – 1957)

At the local level, the civil defence effort would need co-ordinating and the wartime regions created during WW2, were re-instated under the direction of a Regional Commissioner. The Regional

Commissioners were given purpose-built War Rooms which according to the 1949 Working Party would be ...

"Established outside the central key area of its Regional town, it must also be located in an area where adequate signal communications can be provided to keep the War Room in touch with other civil and military headquarters in the region...and with the Central War Room in London."

In practice, the War Rooms were built at the sites of key regional government buildings and cost in the region of £100,000 each to build (at 1950's prices). Building of the War Rooms did not start until 1952 with the War Rooms covering London being built by 1953 and the last to be built in Birmingham in 1956. The War Rooms were designed to accommodate approximately 50 operational staff and including offices specifically for the Regional Commissioner as well as scientific advisers, emergency services (fire, police, medical) and military provision. Sites of the initial War Rooms were located at;

	REGION	**LOCATION**
1	Northern	Newcastle
2	North Eastern	Leeds
3	North Midland	Nottingham
4	Eastern	Cambridge
5	London (North)	Mill Hill
	London (East)	Wanstead
	London (South East)	Chiselhurst
	London (South West)	Cheam
6	Southern	Reading
7	South Western	Bristol
8	Wales	Cardiff
9	Midland	Birmingham
10	North Western	Manchester
11	Scotland	Kirknewton
12	South Eastern	Tunbridge Wells
	Northern Ireland	Belfast

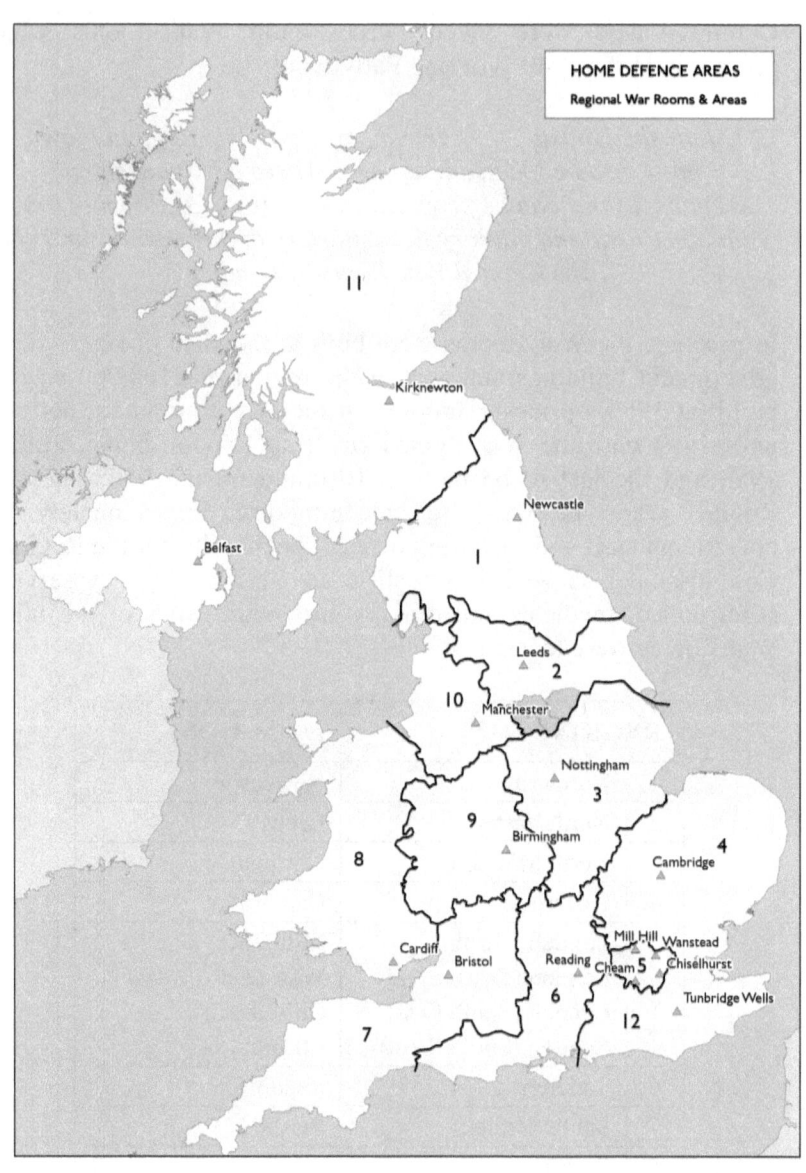

Regional War Rooms & Areas
Source: SYROCM

Regional Seats of Government – RSG (1957 – 1966 / 73)

The 1950s brought new concerns for central and local government planners. Starting in 1953 the increased threat from the Soviet Union as a result of the detonation of their H-Bomb led to a reappraisal of defence plans. War Rooms, which were originally constructed to withstand the effects of between 10 and 20 Hiroshima sized nuclear devices, were seen to be under greater risk from more powerful Soviet nuclear devices. The increasing developments within the Soviet arsenals led planners in the UK to reappraise the effects of an attack on the UK and as a result the War Rooms were soon overtaken in 1955/6 by other plans (although continuing to be used in war exercises until the early 1960s) when larger Regional Seats of Government[5] started to be envisaged.

From the late 1950s, it was now believed that such an attack would have been greater than originally expected and directed towards a greater number of sites within the UK that would have been at the forefront of the UK's retaliatory attack. Airbases, missile sites, military bases and areas of manufacturing and services would have been targets in order to reduce the country's ability to defend itself.

RSG control was seen as key in ensuring effective maintenance of Government control during and after a potential attack on the UK until central government could be restored at the national level. Concerns of the planners were further compounded by the crisis developing in Berlin culminating in the construction of the so-called "anti-fascist" wall and stand-off on Friedrichstraße in 1961 and the Cuban Missile Crisis in 1962.

Although the idea of regional sites was introduced in the late 1950s, it was not until 1962 as a result of a NATO exercise when sites were operating effectively under set operating procedures. Like the previous War Rooms; the sites would have been

---

[5] At this stage however it has to be stressed that Regional Seats of Government relates to the process of control for regionalised Government rather than an actual site or building. This later point did however materialise with sites being chosen to undertake this process being known as Regional Controls from 1957.

controlled by the Regional Commissioner who would automatically assume power of the regional area after a nuclear attack. Their role was to ensure the continuation of government within their designated area along with the maintaining of law and order and effective control and management of all resources. In total the Regional Commissioners would have control of approximately 450 staff[6].

In a document produced by the anti-war group "Spies for Peace" in 1963 which "leaked" the existence of the RSGs to the public after the group successfully entered RSG Site 6 at Warren Row; identified the following resources at RSG sites and each would have had a number of key staff designated as controllers working within these areas;

- Armed Forces (RAF, Army & Navy)[7]
- Emergency Services (Fire, Police & Health)
- Civil Defence
- BBC & Central Office of Information (COI)
- Telecommunications
- Ministry of Agriculture, Fisheries and Food (MAFF)
- Ministries of Transport and Housing

The locations of all the RSGs locations were identified as:-

---

[6] FOI Document relating to 'Money for Regional Seats of Government and Sub Regions': Dated 29th October 1962

[7] The military would have a major role in preserving law and order and the RSG would serve as the District Headquarters for the armed forces under the Regional Military Commander.

	REGION	LOCATION
1	Northern	Catterick Camp
2	North Eastern	York (Imphal Barracks)
3	North Midlands	Nottingham
4	Eastern	Cambridge
5	South Eastern	Dover Castle
6	Southern	Warren Row
7	South Western	Bolt Head
8	Wales	Brecon Barracks
9	Midland	Drakelow
10	North Western	Preston
	Scotland	Edinburgh
	Northern Ireland	Armagh (Gough Barracks)

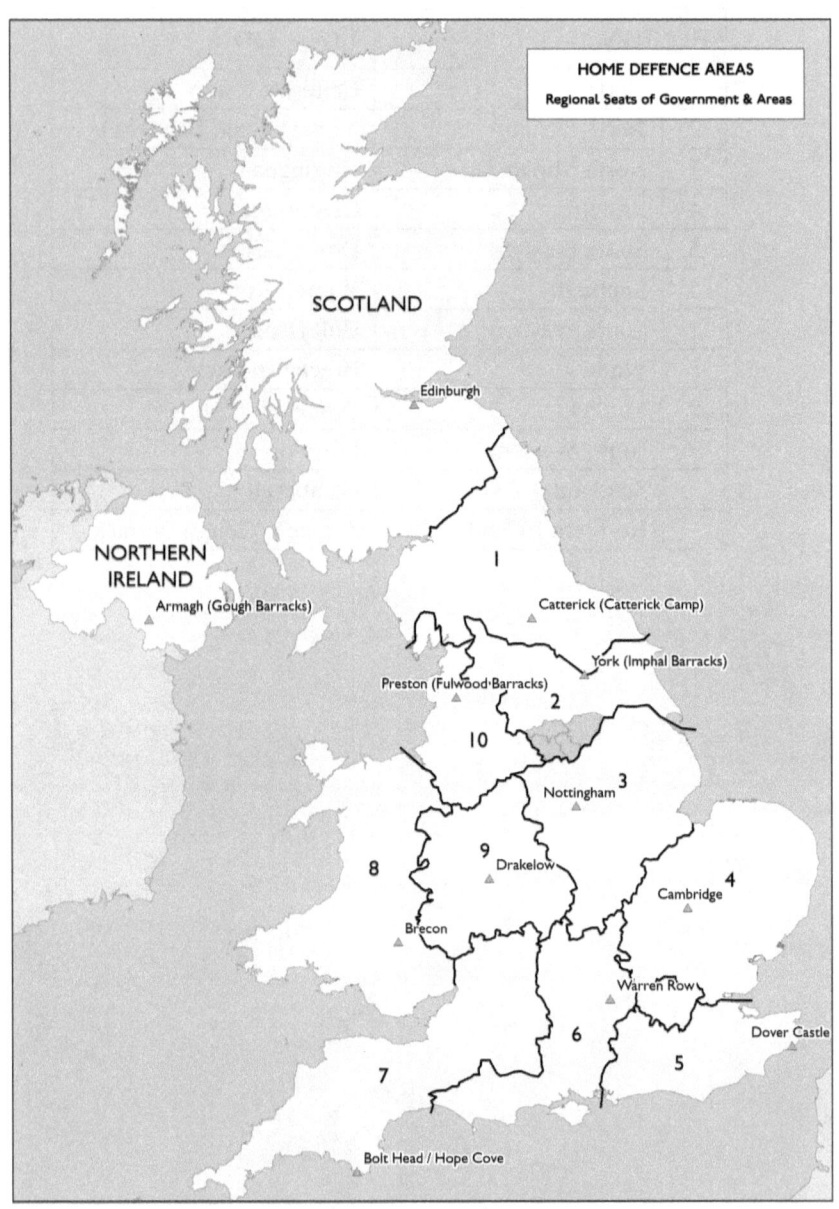

Regional Seats of Government Sites & Region Areas
Source: SYROCM

It must be stressed, that the term "Regional Seats of Government" don't necessarily refer to an actual building i.e. bunker, as one would envisage, but in fact related more to the formation of an effective team of staff that would come together to govern a specific region in the aftermath of a nuclear war on the UK.

Sites were identified during the early 1960s as Regional Seats of Government and these did consist of actual sites of protected accommodation for Governmental staff however with the move to Sub Regional Controls during mid 1960s and the later move to actual Sub Regional HQs during the early 1970s (see later) these were deemed to provide improved links with county and borough controls (to provide operations during the initial lifesaving and survival stage) with the structure of the Regional Seats of Government falling back to a more administrative role which would have taken up residence at such sub regional controls / HQs which ever were felt to offer the least risk to the effective control of regional government AFTER the attack.

Sub-Regional Controls – SRC (1956 – 1965 & 1966 – 1973)

Before RSGs had been delivered, the roles of smaller sub-regional controls were being envisaged. Sub-Regional Controls were initially planned in 1956. These were deemed necessary to co-ordinate rescue in the aftermath of an attack especially within a number of densely populated industrial areas, where it was anticipated that there would be significant destruction in the event of an attack. Although much of the initial planning had been undertaken for the development of these initial Sub-Regional Controls by 1958 only 11 of 19 controllers had been appointed and staffing and premises were yet to be developed.[8]

By 1960 a small number of sub-regional sites were starting to be developed and exercises undertaken to evaluate operational effectiveness, and later in 1962, communications between the Home Office Civil Defence Department and Treasury indicate that

---

[8] Source – Fox, S: Struggle for Survival [ONLINE].

such sites have been developed[9]. Where Regional Controls were developed to manage government for the whole region, these Sub-Regional Controls provided improved liaison with the County and Borough Controls lower down in the communication and operational chain.

By 1963 the benefits of sub-controls were being realised, especially in their assessed effective coordination of operations within the region. The introduction of a Civil Defence Circular (CDC17/63) in this year, stressed that there was a significant lack of any effective plans to organise local administration after the initial "life-saving" phase though and into the "survival" phase. Although the initial focus would still be to provide life saving facilities to "survivors" (food, water, shelter and medical assistance)

The circular laid down:-

- A framework of administration to coordinate and use remaining resources in the best way to keep the rest of the population alive.
- A structure for maintaining law and order.
- Plans for the restoration of a more normal life.

Furthermore; the effectiveness of the initial sub-regions system, highlighted through defence exercises, stressed the need for the similar system to be spread across the country, and not just focused within industrial sub-regions. This therefore necessitated a reappraisal of the sub-regions throughout the United Kingdom and a reassessment of Sub-Regional Control locations. As a result by 1965, the recently elected Labour government ordered a fundamental review of home defence.

One of the main driving forces for this review was to assess the potential for cost savings; however, further defence studies highlighted a greater need for effectiveness to respond to a shortened "precautionary" stage". The plan therefore was to focus only on a network of "permanent" Sub Regional Controls rather

---

[9] FOI letter between Civil Defence Department of the Home Office and HM Treasury Dated: 5th January 1962.

than a network of Regional Seats of Government with the sub regional controls being staffed in the pre-attack period. The Regional Seats would still exist but would form an "administrative" control which would be initiated within the Sub Regional sites as and when central regionalised government control was required.

At regional level, these "new" Sub-Regional Controls were deemed essential to organise government control above local authority level after a nuclear attack while at local level such Sub-Regional Controls provided effective links with local authorities and aimed to;

- Provide help and assistance to local authorities deemed to be overwhelmed with the current situation.
- Deploy resources over a wider area than a county.
- Provide a link to, and assist utility organisations (electricity, water, communications, transport etc) in, the maintenance or resumption of power and water supplies, transport food and other essential services.
- Assist in the overall command and control of the armed forces, fire, police and medical services.

REGION		SUB REGION	LOCATION
1	North	1_1	Carlisle Castle ... or
		1_1	Catterick Camp
		1_2	Shipton
2	North Eastern	2_1	Ilkley, Craiglands Hotel ... or
		2_1	Shipton
		2_2	Conisbrough
		2_3	York (Imphal Barracks)
3	North Midland	3_1	Matlock (County Council)
		3_2	Skendleby
		3_3	Corby (Civic Centre)
4	Eastern	4_1	Bawburgh
		4_2	Kelvedon Hatch
		4_3	Hertford
5	South Eastern	5_1	Dover Castle
		5_2	Guildford
6	Southern	6_1	Warren Row
		6_2	Winchester Prison ... then
		6_2	Basingstoke (1970)
7	South Western	7_1	Ullenwood
		7_2	Hope Cove
8	Wales	8_1	Brecon
		8_2	Bridgend
9	Midland	9_1	Swynnerton
		9_2	Kidderminster
10	North Western	10_1	Preston ... to be replaced with
		10_1	Southport (Duke's House)
		10_2	Hack Green
11	Northern Ireland		Armagh
	Scotland	North	Anstruther
		East	Kirknewton
		West	East Kilbride
		Central	Barnton Quarry

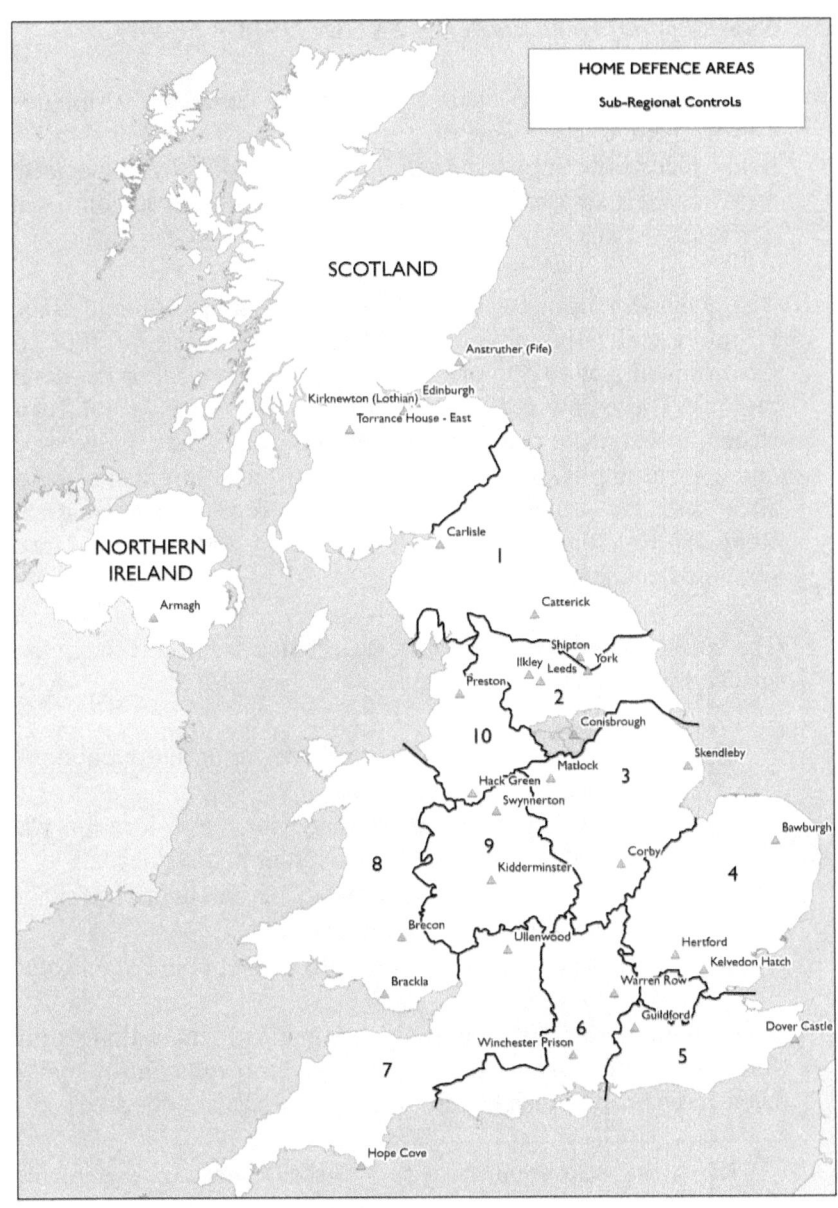

Sub Regional Control Sites (1950s / 60s) & Regional Areas
Source: Fox, S: Struggle for Survival [ONLINE]

Sub-Regional Headquarters – SRHQs (1973 – 1985)

1973 saw a further change to the Regionalised structure of Government in the event of a nuclear war. Increasing focus was being placed on Sub-Regional controls individually; especially in terms of their assessed capability to provide improved control after a potential attack.

The disbandment of the Civil Defence Corps in 1968 and changes to the Local Government boundaries as a result of the Local Government Act 1972[10] saw a need for a reappraisal of the defence regions. These new defence regions were based on the sub-regions structure that had existed throughout the past decade, however cost and control implications led to an overall reduction in sub-regional sites from the previous 23 to 17 and were redesignated as Sub-Regional Headquarters (SRHQs). Scotland and Northern Ireland remained unchanged.

The role of this SRHQ network was focused on the life-saving & survival phase and aimed to;

- Obtain, process and disseminate information about the extent and effect of the attack.
- Determine priorities and arrange for the re-location where appropriate, of resources to meet immediate needs.
- Prepare the administrative groundwork for the establishment of regional government.
- Co-operate and support the activities of county controllers.

The changes in 1973 initially maintained the administrative function of the dispersed Regional government control that had been progressed during the late 1960s. This consisted of the

---

[10] The Local Government Act abolished previous existing local government structures, and created a two-tier system of counties and districts everywhere. Some of the new counties were designated metropolitan counties, containing metropolitan boroughs instead. The allocation of functions differed between the metropolitan and the non-metropolitan areas (the so-called 'shire counties') — for example, education and social services were the responsibility of the shire counties, but in metropolitan counties this was given to the boroughs.

dispersal of Regional Commissioner and staff around the region within the "pre-attack" phase and then to establish Regional controls at a location in each region that offered the best surviving communications and accommodation for the purpose. In essence this process was less fluid, with regional teams gradually being focused onto a single site.

REGION		SUB REGION	LOCATION
1	North	1_1	Hexham
2	North Eastern	2_1	Shipton
3	North Midland	3_1 3_2	Skendleby Loughborough
4	Eastern	4_1 4_2	Bawburgh Hertford
5	London	5_1	Guildford Kelvedon Hatch
6	Southern	6_1 6_2	Dover Castle Basingstoke
7	South Western	7_1 7_2	Ullenwood Hope Cove
8	Wales	8_2	Bridgend
9	Midland	9_1 9_2	Swynnerton Drakelow
10	North Western	10_1 10_2	Southport Hack Green
11	Northern Ireland		Armagh
	Scotland	North East West Central	Anstruther Kirknewton East Kilbride Barnton Quarry

Sub Regional Control Sites (1970s) & Regional Areas
Source: SYROCM

Regional Government Headquarters – RGHQs (1985 – 1990s)

The previous incarnation of Regional Government at the beginning of the 1980s swung from the previous administrative role to the final change being to a network of key protected sites similar to that was created with the Regional Seats of Government during the late 1950s through to the late 1960s.

These sites were generally based upon the former Sub-Regional Headquarters' sites and were generally refurbished for their new role, however a number of new RGHQ sites[11] were constructed or other sites reutilised. For instance new RGHQs were investigated / set up at a number of former Royal Observer Corps Group / Sector Controls buildings[12] to replace sites unsuitable for the new RGHQ role. The sites which were designated as RGHQs from 1985 are shown in the table below.

The role of the Regional Commissioner would form the main responsibility for the governing of the region if Central Government were unable to operate as expected and would be based at one of the sub regional sites within their region. A deputy regional commissioner would occupy the other site to ensure that the regional management and governmental control was maintained in the event of one of the sites being put out of action.

Depending upon which site was used; all communication links from the county government levels would have been directed to one of the RGHQ forming the operational base. Working with the sub regions and county / local emergency controls, the RGHQ role would have been to manage the administration of government including:

---

[11] Crowborough in Sussex was a new build to replace Dover Castle in Region 6 and Chilmark in Wiltshire replaced Ullenwood in Region 7. A further new build was at Cultybraggan in Scotland and was operational from 1990.

[12] Former ROC Group Controls at Bedford, Lawford Heath, Wrexham and the former UKWMO HQ at Goosnargh nr Preston were investigated as possible RGHQ sites.

- Assessing and guiding priorities between county and borough controls
- The control of broadcasting especially to inform the population within the region.
- Law and order through the assistance from the police and to ensure that some form of justice system was maintained.
- Allocation of assistance from the armed forces,
- Co-ordination of the survival and recovery of the nation under central government control.

The role of the non executive Regional commissioner was only to be of an administrative nature. The actual governing and management of the population based on these and general life-saving actions would still lie with the county / borough controls.

REGION		SUB REGION	LOCATION
1	Scotland	1.1	Anstruther
			Cultybraggan (from 1990)
		1.2	Kirknewton
2	North Eastern	2.1	Shipton
		2.2	Hexham
3	North Midland	3.1	Skendleby
		3.2	Loughborough
4	Eastern	4.1	Bawburgh
		4.2	Hertford / Bedford
5	London	5.1	Kelvedon Hatch
6	Southern	6.1	Crowborough
		6.2	Basingstoke
7	South Western	7.1	Chilmark
		7.2	Hope Cove
8	Wales	8.1	*Llandudno Junction*[13]
		8.1	*Wrexham (from 1992)*
		8.2	Bridgend
9	Midland	9.1	Swynnerton
		9.2	Drakelow
		9.2	*Lawford Heath (from 1992)*
10	North Western	10.1	Southport
		10.2	Hack Green
11	Northern Ireland	11.1	Belfast (to 1989/90)
			Ballymena (From 1989/90)

---

[13] It was planned that Wales would consist of two regional zones (8.1 and 8.2). In fact, Wales only had the one site, located at Bridgend (Brackla) (Zone 8.2). Work initially started on a site located at a former WW2 cold store at Llandudno Junction in North Wales (8.1 Region Area) however increasing costs led to the abandonment of this site in 1986 and it was not until 1992 (after the Cold War) that North Wales gained its RGHQ 8.1 in the guise of the former ROC group HQ located at Wrexham.

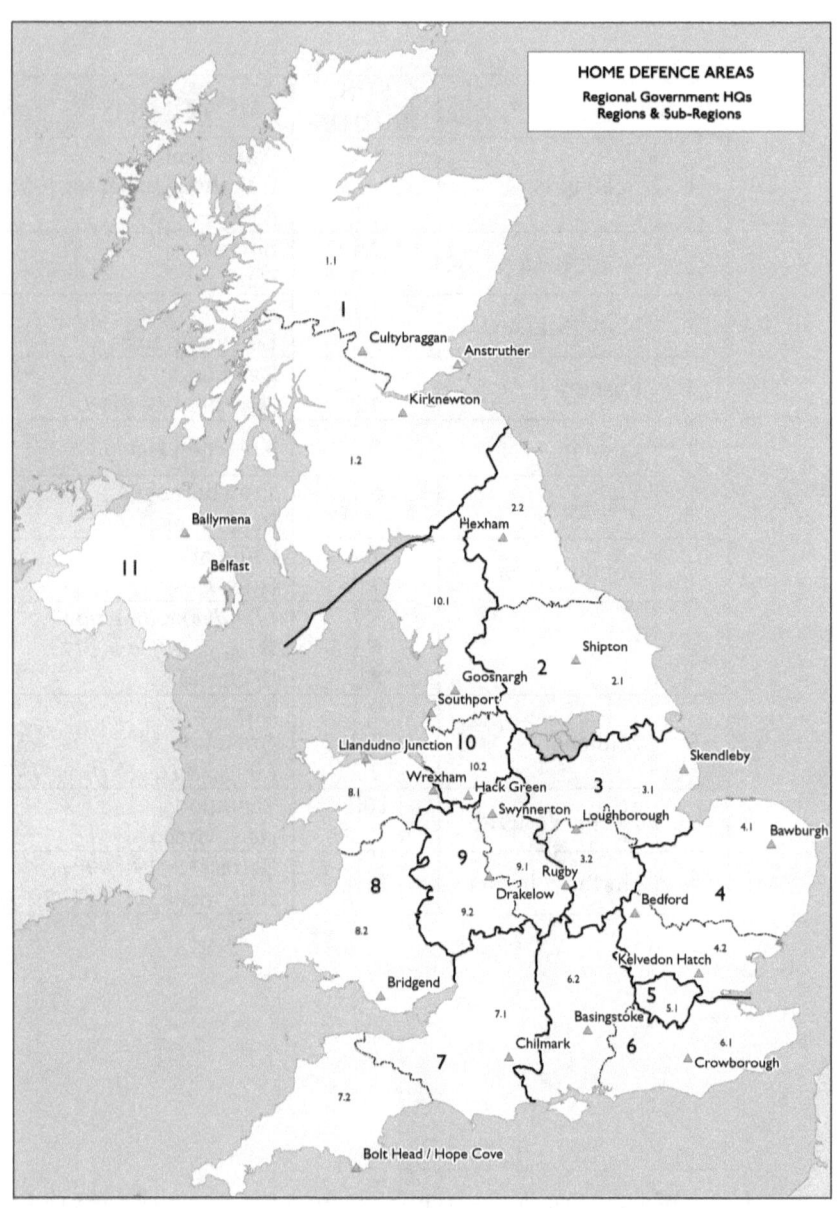

Regional Government Headquarters Sites & Region Areas
Source: SY ROC Museum

CHAPTER 3
LOCAL GOVERNMENT

Civil Defence Planning Regulations placed on local Authorities (County, Borough, Parish etc) the responsibility to make plans in peacetime to provide for the essential needs of people in war, and also to carry out these plans if required to do so. The process of civil(ian) protection (or defence) was therefore seen by Local Authorities as being essentially humanitarian since it aimed to meet the needs for everyday services provided in peacetime such as water, sewerage, medical facilities, production of food, energy, transport and communications.

Local Authorities viewed the future war to take a variety of forms ranging from air strikes with high accuracy conventional weapons to the devastating consequences of all-out strategic nuclear attack. A developing war crisis, with such an implied nuclear threat was seen to have the potential to cause the breakdown of society through widespread fear and apprehension. This ultimately would lead to a mass exodus from supposed target areas, and lead to public disorder and absenteeism; effects which were seen to result in the partial failure of public services and loss of control by the authorities.

It was expected that the use of conventional non-nuclear weapons would have been directed towards military targets such as air bases, army barracks and other key strategic military installations. The effects of such were seen as temporary rather than permanent. Areas that were free from attack would most probably have been unaffected. The consequences of a strategic nuclear attack would however be more severe. The effects of a nuclear explosion with its generated heat flash and blast wave would have caused heavy loss of life, damage and disruption on a wide scale to government, industry, commerce and communications.

Furthermore; no part of the country would have been unaffected by the subsequent radioactive fallout which would have been deposited anywhere in the country as a result of a nuclear ground burst sucking ground dirt and debris into the air and travelling on prevailing winds. Even so, people would have been able to survive the attack's immediate effects and much of the country could be expected to be capable of supporting life, albeit under conditions which might be primitive by current standards.

Three hazards were seen to impact upon the continuing survival of these people. These consist of;

- Violence and Public Disorder
- Disease
- Waste of Resources

The education of the population in these three areas was seen to have significant benefit, with the belief that if survivors are aware of these hazards and know about the ways in which they can be tackled, then their chances of survival would be considerably enhanced.

Voluntary Dispersal of People

The Government outlined a scheme for the voluntary dispersal of people in certain priority classes i.e. women and children, from areas of major population and Local Authorities were asked to prepare detailed plans identifying how such a dispersal scheme would have been developed within their area. These plans would have provided for the assembly of persons within the designated dispersal area and for their movement to main departure points and billeting[14] centres from which they would have been taken to their billets.

Authorities of Control

County Control

The County structure of control was to be headed at local authority level by a controller with a small advisory Emergency Committee

---

[14] A billeting centre provides accommodation for evacuees from the dispersal area.

of elected members and staffed by Local Authority officials and liaison representatives similar to those at Zone Headquarters.

District Control

The District Control was to be headed by a controller with a small advisory Emergency Committee of elected members and staffed by Local Authority officials with liaison officers from certain Government Departments, Public Utilities and Industry.

Parish / Community Control

Parishes or lower level community control were prepared to act independently for as long as necessary and should support a leader acting on their behalf. Community Advisers were required to assist and advise the chosen leader.

SECTION 3
"ASSISTING GOVERNMENT"

TO RECAP ...

The previous chapter explains the need for Government control at both a regional and local level in order to provide effective control of the country and regions before, during and after a nuclear attack. The chapter identified a systematic chain of command structure that existed throughout the cold war period ranging from the administrative government control at Regional level through to local coordination at Local and District levels. Undertaking the processes within this chain of command requires a vast amount of information and assistance from a number of organisations. These organisations aimed to provide information for government decision making such as:-

- the impact of the nuclear attack,
- levels of damage
- potential numbers of survivors
- safe areas to direct rescue services etc.

... or aim to provide physical assistance such as ...

- rescue and survivor assistance
- medical care
- maintenance of law and order
- maintenance of utility services (water, electricity and telecommunications)

This section therefore concentrates on the main organisations involved in these areas. These were:-

- Royal Observer Corps[15]
- Civil Defence Corps (including Auxiliary Fire Service)
- Utility companies

---

[15] In the case of the Royal Observer Corps' history from before World War II to 1995, has been included in order to provide context.

CHAPTER 4
ROYAL OBSERVER CORPS

"Forewarned is Forearmed" – The Beacon System

> *"And on, and on, without a pause, untired they bounded still*
> *All night from tower to tower they sprang; they sprang from hill to hill*
>
> *Till the proud Peak unfurled the flag o'er Darwin's rocky dales*
> *Till like volcanoes flared to heaven the stormy hills of Wales,*
>
> *Till twelve fair counties saw the blaze on Malvern's lonely height,*
> *Till streamed in crimson on the wind the Wrekin's crest of light"*

Prior to the aeroplane the greatest fear of attack was from the sea. Fire beacons to warn of attack have been used since primitive times to warn of impending attack and the same idea formed the basis of the ROCs modus operandi. Although the use of signalling by fire has its origins going back to the Romans, the main development and use of fire in the form of lighted beacons was during the reign of Edward II (1307-1327) when fire signals were used on the Isle of Wight to warn of the return of his wife Queen Isabella who conspired with the English Barons to dethrone him.

It was however not until 1372 when a system of organised warning beacons on high points across the country, was ordered by Edward IV to warn ports and signify a call to arms for the "countywide" spread of militia in the event of invasion of the country. "Bekyns" as they were initially known were deemed to provide a far faster and effective warning "message" than a messenger struggling along difficult and dangerous tracks on horseback. Sites were located on high ground in which they could be seen from great distance and hence hills, castles and church roofs formed the favourite locations, however horsemen were held in reserve if visibility was poor.

Signalling Beacon
Source: SYROCM

Such sites were managed on a regular basis with local Shires having the responsibility for maintenance, provision of materials to generate the fires[16] and to pay the watchers who kept a 24-hour "watch" during the majority of the year[17]. The system was not, however, foolproof and when in 1545 as a result of rumours spreading of a French invasion on the South Coast, beacons were lit; the Worcestershire militia consisting of an army of labourers and farm-workers, often armed with nothing more than a scythe or an axe, tramped all the way to Swindon before they were told it was a false alarm.

---

[16] Materials usually consisted of wood soaked in tar, flax or pitch and were concentrated in an iron basket on the top of a pole.

[17] The watch season was held between Ascension day (40th day after Easter Sunday) and Feast of St Michael (Michaelmas – 29th September) and the 24-hour watch involved 2 persons during the day and 3 at night.

The Spanish Armada

King Philip II of Spain had been king consort of England until the death, in 1558, of his wife, Queen Mary I of England, and he took exception to the policies pursued by her successor, his sister-in-law Elizabeth I. The aim of his expedition was to invade and conquer England, thereby suppressing support for the United Provinces – that part of the Spanish Netherlands in possession of the Dutch rebels – and cutting off attacks by the English against Spanish possessions in the New World and against the Atlantic treasure fleets. The king was supported by Pope Sixtus V, who treated the invasion as a crusade; with the promise of a further subsidy should the Armada make land.

On 28th May 1588 the Spanish Armada set sail from Lisbon, headed for the English Channel. The fleet consisted of approximately:-

- 130 ships.
- 8,000 sailors & 18,000 soldiers.
- 1,500 brass & 1,000 iron guns.

It was not until 19th July 1588 however, when the Spanish Armada was seen sailing up the English Channel from a watch post located at the top of St Michael's Mount near Penzance, Cornwall. From this moment the network of beacons which had been set up on the hilltops, church towers and castles along the South Coast were lit to warn of the threat of the incoming Spanish invasion. News of the invasion was conveyed to London which gave extra time to organise retaliatory forces.

On 29th July 1588 the two fleets met in battle off Gravelines. The English emerged victorious from the battle even though Spanish losses were not great; three ships were sunk, one captured, and four more ran aground. As a result of this defeat, the Duke of Medina Sedonia decided that the Armada must return to Spain. The English blocked the Channel, so that the only route open to the Spanish was north around the tip of Scotland, and down the coast of Ireland. It was then that the unpredictable British weather took a hand in the proceedings. A succession of storms scattered the Spanish ships, resulting in shipwrecks and heavy losses.

By the time the tattered Armada regained Spain, it had lost half its ships and three-quarters of its men. In England the victory was greeted as a sign of divine approval for the Protestant cause. The storms that scattered the Armada were seen as intervention by God with 'services of thanks' being held throughout the country, and a commemorative medal struck, with the words inscribed;

"God blew and they were scattered"

The war continued for a further fifteen years. The beacon system along the South Coast was hailed as a success and formed the main focus of further beacons across the country during this period and as a basis for warning of further invasion during the subsequent war with France in 1792.

It is from the operational success of this network of beacons that the badge of the Royal Observer Corps is derived; depicting a Beacon Lighter of Elizabethan times and utilising the old adage "Forewarned is Forearmed".

R.O.C. (Kings Crown) Badge depicting Elizabethan Beacon Lighter

The War Years – WW1 to WW2

World War 1

The ROC had its beginnings during World War I. At the beginning of the war the need for an air raid warning system was not envisaged as air flight was still in its infancy and the overall threat from aerial bombs was not deemed significant; however, as raids by Zeppelin airships increased during 1915 situations changed indicating that a warning system was required that provided an indication of the movements of hostile aircraft. Information was therefore required for defence purposes as well as for air raid warnings.

The system of defences were initially placed under the control of the Admiralty who arranged with the Police to telephone any reports of any aircraft heard or seen within an area of approximately 60 miles of London. Later, this area was extended to include the Isle of White, Hampshire, East Anglia, Northamptonshire and Oxfordshire. At the same time the War Office instructed Chief Constables to forward similar messages to them by telegram.

Eventually the system was extended to cover the whole of England and Wales and at the same time reporting lines were structured to reduce duplication of information, so that reports were passed to the Admiralty who would then forward directly to the War Office. The reliance on the telephone system of this system however led to significant problems of network congestion.

By 1916 the War Office had taken control of the system, creating a more regular system of observers and creating a series of cordons outside vulnerable areas. The observers were organised within a series of some 200 posts established in strategic areas. These posts were simple constructions generally consisting of emplacements surrounded by sand-bags. This reporting system formed the basis of the "Metropolitan Observation Service" for the London area, as this was considered to be the main target area for enemy attacks. The move towards replacing the police with military personnel eventually was proved unsatisfactory as the men were deemed to be of 'poor intelligence' and of 'worse discipline'. Eventually, the military personnel were replaced by the police who passed observations of enemy zeppelins through to the Admiralty using the public telephone system. The Admiralty collated all the information gathered from the posts in some detail and forwarded the information through to Air defence sites. This system proved to be reasonably successful in combating the Zeppelin.

Early in 1917 however, Germany started to introduce fixed wing aircraft as more versatile strategic bomber to attack the UK. On 25th May 1917 a Gotha G.IV bomber dropped its first bomb over Folkestone. Following this attack the number of airship raids decreased rapidly in favour of raids by the fixed wing Gotha G.IV / G.V and the aircraft much larger "Riesenflugzeug" (giant aircraft); the Staaken RVI, bomber before Zeppelin raids were called off entirely.

To answer this new threat Major General E B Ashmore was appointed to devise an improved system of detection, communication and control. Major General Ashmore was a trained pilot and had been in command of the 29th artillery division in Belgium. Having assessed the system, Ashmore identified that police messages were being received in London in as little time as three minutes; however the average delay was deemed to be greater. He also noted that no reports from an area could not always be taken to mean that there were no bombers in that area.

By early 1918 he started to devise a system which made use of all the various existing defence units which covered closely the London and South / South Eastern districts. The system; known as the London Air Defence Area (L.A.D.A) was fully operational by September 1918 and brought together units comprising coastal and inland observation posts, searchlight and gun stations; balloon aprons, aerodromes and emergency landing grounds into coordinated groups of twos and threes and which were connected to 25 Sub-Controls. Reports from the units were fed through to the centres and then onwards from the centres through to Major General Ashmore's headquarters. As a result, the system met with some success and although it was not fully working until September 1918 (the last air raid took place on 19th May 1918) the lessons learnt provided valuable grounding for the later development of the Corps.

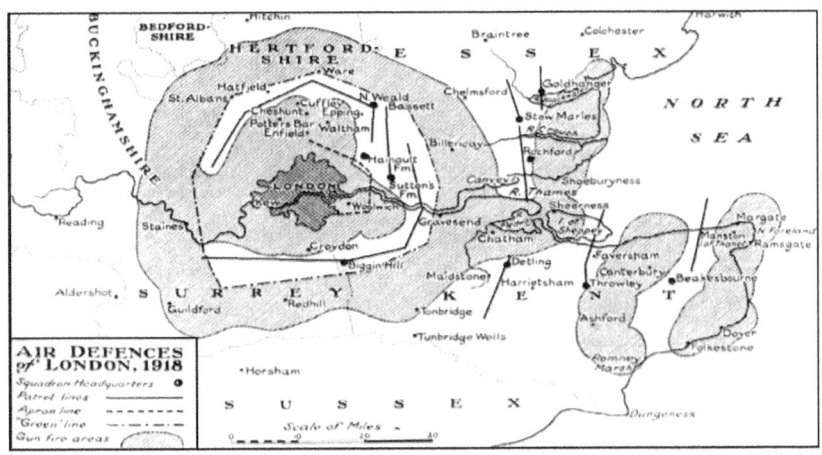

Ashmore's London Air Defence Area (L.A.D.A) as operational from 1918

The peace after World War 1 was followed by a period of strict economy and limited armament. In January 1924, an inquiry was held to investigate the aerial defence of the south east of England, south of a line drawn from Portland Bill to the Wash. As a result of this inquiry it was decided that an organised system was essential for the rapid collection and distribution of information on the movement of hostile and friendly aircraft.

	Air Raids		
	Aeroplanes	Airships	Deaths
1914	3	0	0
1915	4	42	186
1916	28	126	302
1917	341	30	650
1918	59	10	178
Total	**435**	**208**	**1316**

Statistics of Air Raids on the UK during WW1

Formation of the Observer Corps

In August and September 1924 the first experiments were organised by Major General Ashmore to assess aircraft movements. It was decided to use the area between the Romney Marshes and Tonbridge and these trials proved satisfactory. So much so that, in the following year, two observation areas was formed to cover the whole of Kent, Sussex and part of Surrey. With the co-operation of the Chief Constables concerned, these two areas were sited with observation posts and plotting centres manned by personnel who had been enrolled as special constables. No.1 Observer Corps group was headquartered in Maidstone and No.2 was based in Horsham with twenty seven posts and sixteen posts respectively under their control. By November 1926 the Observer Corps covered an area extending from Hampshire to the middle of Suffolk, and comprised No's 1 and 2 groups, and No's 3 and 18 groups with the headquarters at Winchester and Colchester respectively.

As the tests carried out proved consistently successful, plans were made by Major General Ashmore to expand the Observer Groups into Hertfordshire, Buckinghamshire with further posts at Harrow and Uxbridge. Although the Corps had made a good start, further expansion to the end of 1929 was slow, with only the 4 groups existing. Also during 1929, control of the Corps was transferred to the Air Ministry with the first commandant appointed to the Corps being Air Commodore E A D Masterman CB CMG CBE AFC RAF (Ret'd). On the 15th May 1931, No. 17 Group, with its centre at Watford, was formed and No. 18 Group was enlarged by the addition of 3 extra observation posts.

Observer Corps Expansion

Over the next 8 years, the political situation in Europe deteriorated with the threat from the growth of German air power and the increasing emergence of faster long-range bombers based in Germany. This rendered it necessary to reorientate the air defence system for Great Britain, which ultimately would impact upon the role of the Observer Corps. It was thought that London would be no longer the main key target of any potential attack. The main focus now of Germany's attack focused on the limiting any potential retaliatory measures by Great Britain.

Key industrial cities located in the Midlands and North such as Birmingham and Sheffield were now deemed possible targets as a result of their key contribution towards any defence retaliation. Bombs, planes and guns all need steel and the Midlands and especially Sheffield played a considerable part in the production of these items. Furthermore, transport systems would be a probable target as these were essential for carrying raw materials into and finished products from these manufacturing areas, but also enabled the transport of food, civilians and armed forces. Any damage to these links would ultimately result in considerable impact on the war effort. As a result, key ports such as Immingham and Hull and especially the railways also formed key targets by German bombers.

On 7th and 10th December 1934, a conference chaired by Air Commodore O.T. Boyd, O.B.E, M.C, A.F.C was held. The findings from this conference were subsequently published in a report by Boyd in January 1935. This report highlighted the need for a considerable expansion of the Corps, greater than by any previous reports. Furthermore; bearing in mind the growing threat from Germany, such developments should be progressed as soon as possible over a four year period with a final completion date for such measures being set at 1st March 1939.

The key outputs from the report recommended;

- A larger geographic area should be covered by the network of observation posts stretching from Middlesbrough in the North through to Poole in the South and controlled by 16 groups (rather than 18 previously recommended in an earlier report in 1924); the main concentration of these new groups being to the east of the country.
- Effective communications should be developed between observation posts and group centres and between group centres and the two RAF fighting area headquarters covering the north and south of the country.

In respect to the former point, four stages of development were identified;

From 1st March 1935	New groups formed at Bedford (12 Group); Oxford (4 Group) and Cambridge (15 Group) and link groups created at Winchester (3 Group); Oxford (4 Group) and Watford (17 group).
From 1st March 1936	New groups created at York (10 Group) and Lincoln (11 Group).
From 1st March 1937	New groups created at Manchester (7 Group); Leeds (8 Group) and York (9 Group)..
From 1st March 1938	New Groups created at Coventry (5 Group) and Derby (6 Group).

The latter point aimed to bring the control of the Observer Corps closer to the Royal Air Force and hence connect the Corps into the RAF's programme of expansion and development of an Air Raid Warning system. This latter system relied to a great degree on the ultimate efficiency of the Corps to supply the necessary quality of information from the Corps posts to the RAF to enable the efficient management and control of its fighters over land.

Munich Crisis

During 1938, the situation within Europe deteriorated sharply with Hitler keen to progress his plans for German expansion, issued an ultimatum to the Chancellor of Austria to resign control of the country and allow a new Chancellor of Germany's choosing to take control. With his back against a wall and considering the ultimate threat of Germanys' troops marching into Austria, the Austrian Chancellor resigned his post. He was replaced by a Nazi sympathiser loyal to Hitler who immediately ordered the Austrian army to offer no resistance to German troops who were invited to enter Austria. As a result, Hitler had achieved his plan for Anschlüss - the union of Austria and Germany.

When Austria became a part of Nazi Germany, Czechoslovakia, a country formed out of the victory of the Western Allies over Germany in the First World War, found itself surrounded on three sides and though Britain and France had barely reacted to the previous Anschlüss, Hitler was well aware that he could not invade Czechoslovakia without a reason.

By May 1938, the situation began to worsen still further with Hitler stating:-

"It is my unshakable will that Czechoslovakia shall be wiped off the map."

… and furthermore instructing his Generals to develop a plan for completing this by October 1st.

The main focus at this time was in relation to the Sudetenland; which was a small section of the Czech Republic which lay on the border of Germany and many of whose inhabitants were of German descent and were resident there since before the land was made part of a newly created Czechoslovakian state after World War 1. Many of the pro-Nazi Sudeten Germans began to apply pressure on the Czech Government through terrorist attacks, marches and rallies in the Sudetenland with added pressure from Germany.

In September 1938, the British Prime Minister, Neville Chamberlain, met with Hitler at his home in Berchtesgaden. Hitler threatened to invade Czechoslovakia unless Britain supported Germany's plans to regain the Sudetenland as part of Germany. After discussing the issue with the Prime Minister of France (Édouard Daladier) and the Czechoslovakian President (Edvard Beneš); Chamberlain informed Hitler that his proposals were unacceptable.

Hitler, keen to regain the former German lands, knew that Britain and France were unwilling to go to war and also thought it unlikely that these two countries would be keen to join up with the Soviet Union, whose totalitarian system the western democracies hated more that Hitler's fascist dictatorship. The premier of Italy, Benito Mussolini who was a close ally of Hitler, therefore suggested to Hitler that one way of solving this issue was to hold a four-power conference of Germany, Britain, France and Italy. This would exclude both Czechoslovakia and the Soviet Union, and therefore increasing the possibility of reaching an agreement and undermine the solidarity that was developing against Germany.

The meeting took place in Munich on 29th September 1938. Desperate to avoid war and anxious to avoid an alliance with Joseph Stalin and the Soviet Union, Neville Chamberlain and Édouard Daladier of France agreed to Germanys request to regain the Sudetenland as part of Germany. On the 30th September 1938, the Munich Agreement was signed transferring the Sudetenland to Germany. As part of this Hitler promised not to make any further territorial demands in Europe. When Czechoslovakia's head of state; Edvard Beneš, protested at this decision, Neville Chamberlain stressed that Britain was unwilling to go to war over the issue of the Sudetenland.

The Munich Agreement was popular with most people in Britain because it appeared to have prevented a war with Germany. However, some politicians, including Winston Churchill and Anthony Eden, criticised the agreement pointing out that not only had the British government behaved dishonourably, and had lost the total support of the Czech Army.

In March, 1939, the German Army seized the rest of Czechoslovakia. In taking this action Hitler had broken the Agreement signed in Munich that previous year. The British prime minister now realised that Hitler could not be trusted and his appeasement policy now came to an end. On 3rd September 1939, Neville Chamberlain announced to the nation that the country was at war with Germany. To some, this was no surprise. Since the mid 1930s, tensions had been developing within Germany and many believed that it was simply a case of not IF but WHEN. This belief had directed operational developments within the Observer Corps through a number of exercises during 1938.

World War: Mobilisation

On 24 August 1939 Chief Constables issued mobilisation notices to all members of the Observer Corps. At this time the administration, recruitment and payment for voluntary members of the Corps was transferred from the Police Force directly to the Air Ministry.

As a result the observers:-

- Relinquished their Special Constable status which formed the initial basis of being a member of the Corps since initial setup.
- Became entitled to a remuneration of 1/3d. per hour, with a maximum of £3 a week and increased to £3 5/- by the award of a 5/- a week War Bonus from 1st July 1940.
- Were given the opportunity for applying for employment on a full time basis (48-hour week) or accepting part time employment.

War was eventually declared on 3 September 1939, with observer posts and centres being manned continuously until the end of the war on the 12th May 1945, four days after VE Day on 8 May 1945. The first months of World War II were known as the Phoney War where there was little significant enemy aircraft activity over Britain however by the end of May 1940, The Battle of Dunkirk started when Allied troops were cut off by the German army in north-east France. This resulted in the evacuation of British troops in "Operation Dynamo" which ended on 4 June. During this time the RAF lost 944 aircraft, half of these being fighters. Observer Corps posts in Kent and around the Thames estuary were able to play some part by observing and plotting aircraft while they were over England. It was however an extremely useful period for training and practice which proved to be extremely valuable within a few months.

"Battle of Britain" & Radar

After the invasion of France, the German aim was air superiority over Britain to be achieved by destroying RAF fighters in the air and on the ground, and by bombing aircraft factories. Winning the "Battle of Britain", as it was soon called, was Germany's prerequisite in preparation for the invasion of Britain known as 'Operation Sealion'. Radar[18], which used electromagnetic waves to

---

[18] Radar – Radio Detection And Ranging

identify the range, altitude, direction, or speed of both moving and fixed objects, had started to gain greater use during WW2, having been experimentally tested during 1935 by inventor Robert Watson-Watt. The British Chain Home radar system was developed and operational by 1940 and formed a ring of coastal radar stations comprising two types of radar:-

- Chain Home stations, or AMES Type 1 (Air Ministry Experimental Station), provided long-range detection.
- Chain Home Low stations, or AMES Type 2, were shorter-ranged but could detect aircraft flying at lower levels

The radar stations[19] was able to provide warning of enemy aircraft approaching the British coast, but once they had crossed the coastline the Observer Corps provided the only means of tracking them through the network of strategically placed observation posts.

During the period from July to October 1940 the Corps was fully stretched 24 hours a day plotting aircraft and passing this essential information to RAF groups and sectors. The Battle of Britain saw the start of the Blitz, the shift of German bombing from airfields to cities; the Observer Corps provided the information which enabled air raid warnings to be issued. The Blitz itself continued until early in the summer of 1941 and bombing on a reduced scale continued until March 1945.

After the successes of 1940 and early 1941 the "Observer Corps" was retitled the "Royal Observer Corps" (the ROC) and although it was to continue as a civilian organisation it was to be administered by the Royal Air Force, and for the first time women members were recruited. Members of both sexes were employed in two forms: Class A who was required to work for 56 hours a week, and Class B members who undertook up to 24 hours duty per week. For the rest of the war the ROC continued to provide an essential part of Britain's air defences.

---

[19] Germany had also developed radar and which was deemed to be more advanced than that in use in Britain. Their system however was developed for use at sea and was deemed to be less integrated and therefore was not so much of a problem to the RAF.

"Seaborne"

On the 6th June 1944, the largest amphibious assault in history was launched against the Normandy coast – its ultimate goal was the establishment of an allied foothold in Nazi-occupied France. During preparations for this invasion; (commonly known as D-Day and code named "Operation Overlord"), the Air Ministry issued a confidential order A63/1944, which consisted of the proposals for the Royal Observer Corps to participate in the forthcoming Operations. The order outlined an urgent need for a substantial number of "expert" ROC Observers to be employed on recognition duties in defensively-equipped merchant ships. Their initial role was to advise as to the identity of aircraft at sea. This role was deemed to be only advisory, and responsibility for accepting or rejecting the advice and taking any necessary action rested with the ship's captain.

Over 1,000 candidates applied to join as Seaborne Observers of which approximately 800 were selected to perform the seaborne duties. Under the leadership of Group Commandant C.G. Cooke, these "Seaborne" Observers were trained at the Royal Bath Hotel in Bournemouth before temporarily joining the Royal Navy with the rank of Petty Officer (Aircraft Identifier). They continued to wear their ROC uniforms, but wore Seaborne shoulder flashes and a Royal Navy brassard with the letters 'RN'.

During the D-Day Landings two Seaborne observers were allocated to each warship of the U.S. Navy and the defensively equipped merchant ships and were duly given control of each ship's anti-aircraft battery, thereby reducing any risk of friendly fire incidents, which had previously been at a relatively high level. In total over the period of the operation, only two observers lost their lives; 22 survived their ships being sunk and a number being injured during the landings. The Seaborne operation was seen as an unqualified success and was recognised by His Majesty King George VI, by the approval of the use of "Seaborne" shoulder titles as a permanent feature of the observer uniform. After the invasion and just before his death Air Chief Marshall Trafford Leigh Mallory wrote the following to be circulated to all ROC personnel.

"I have reports from both pilots and naval officers regarding the Seaborne volunteers who have more than fulfilled their duties and have undoubtedly saved many of our aircraft from being engaged by our ships guns ..."

"... I should be grateful if you would please convey to all ranks of the Royal Observer Corps, and in particular to the Seaborne Observers themselves, how grateful I and all pilots in the Allied Expeditionary Air Force are, for their assistance, which has contributed in no small measure to the safety of our own aircraft, and also to the efficient protection of the ships at sea ...".

" ... The work of the Royal Observer Corps is quite unjustly overlooked, and on this occasion be as advertised as possible, and all units of the Air Defence of Great Britain are therefore to be informed of the success of this latest venture of the Royal Observer Corps".

On 12 May 1945, when it was certain that all Luftwaffe aircraft were grounded, the ROC temporarily stood down, to be re-activated in January 1947 to meet post-war threats.

Corps' Structure during WW2

The headquarters of each group was operated from a Centre and it controlled about 30 to 40 Posts. Each of these would be some 8 km to 13 km (5 to 8 miles) from its neighbour. By the end of the war in 1945 there were some 40 centres covering England, Wales and Scotland, controlling in total approximately 1,560 observer posts. The ROC did not operate in Northern Ireland until 1954. The posts within the South Yorkshire area reported directly to the Leeds 8 Group control, which was based initially at Leeds GPO building on Vicar Lane and then by 1941 at Grove House, Hyde Park, Leeds.

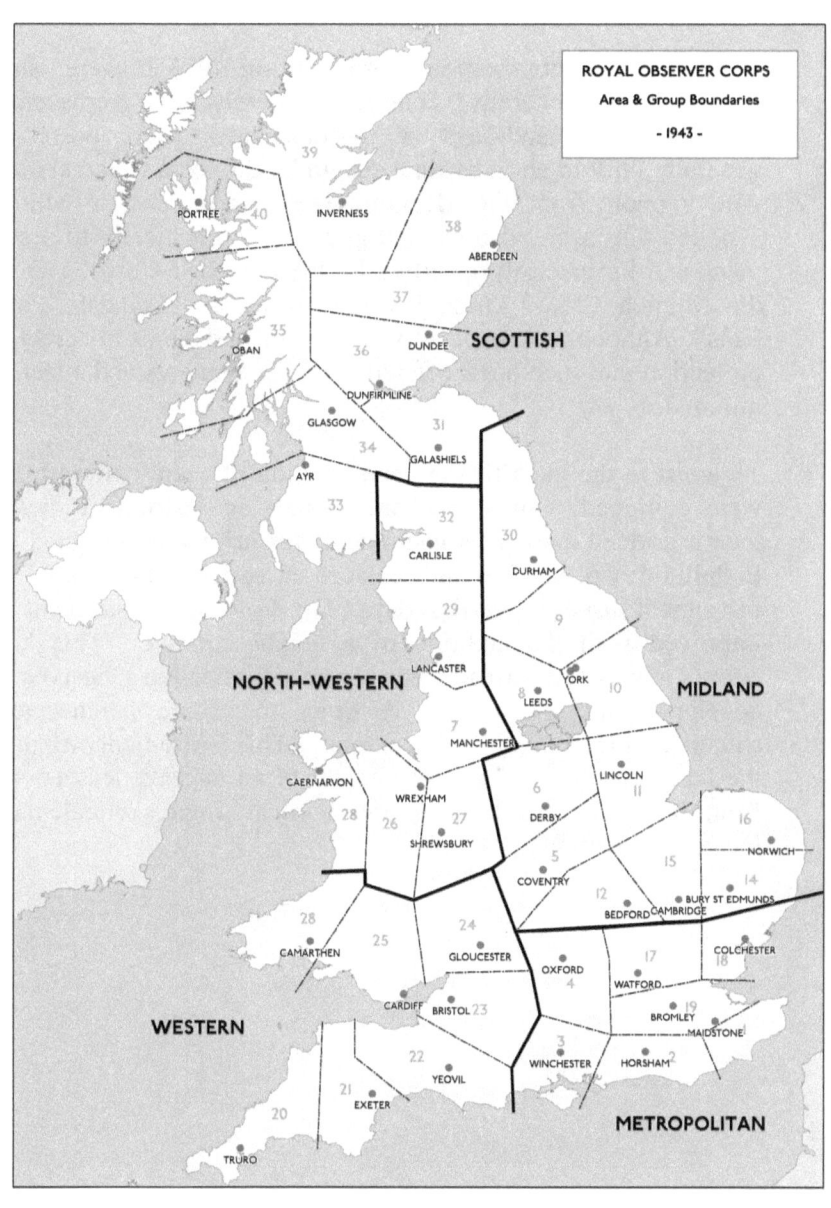

Area & Group Boundaries during WW2
Source: SYROCM

"WW2 era" Aircraft Observation Posts

Early aircraft observation posts during WW2 were simple constructions generally consisting merely of emplacements surrounded by sand-bags or wooden huts. These posts were generally built to an individual design by the local observers albeit with support from the General Headquarters or Air Ministry. Wooden huts were also erected and were built locally to a set of plans and in materials specified by the Observer Corps' HQ after the Munich Crisis. These became known as "Standard Pattern Huts". Although such posts were cheap and quick to erect, the protection that such posts offered from the elements and attack was minimal.

To assist in the identification and location of enemy aircraft, Posts were equipped with a mechanical sighting instrument mounted over a gridded map. This instrument was originally designed by R B Pullin & Co. in 1934 and replaced an earlier "pantograph" type instrument used in earlier days. By 1940 the instrument was improved with the addition of a height corrector. This height corrector was known as a 'Micklethwait' after the Observer who developed and patented it in order to enable heights to be calculated more easily and accurately. This instrument worked on the basis that if you knew the height of an aircraft, it is possible, from its horizontal bearing and vertical angle, to calculate a locational position.

The ROC Post Instrument as used for the locating of enemy and friendly aircraft
(Source: ROC Training Manual 1951)

After setting the instrument with an estimate of the aeroplane's height, the observer would align a sighting bar with the aircraft. This bar was mechanically connected to a vertical pointer which would indicate the position of the aircraft on the map. Observers in posts reported the map coordinates, height and number of aircraft for each sighting to their Centre. The initial estimations of heights were corrected during plots through communication between the Centre and other posts in the area using triangulation between other posts sightings or direct report of a planes location directly above a post.

At each Centre plotters sat around a large table map, they had head sets continuously connected to a Cluster of posts, usually three in number. The plotting table consisted of a large map with grid squares and posts marked. Counters were placed on the map at the reported positions, each of which indicated the height and the number of aircraft represented, a colour coding system indicated the time of observation in 5 minute segments. The table was surrounded by plotters, each communicating with a cluster of posts. Over time the tracks of aircraft could be traced, the colour coding enabled the extrapolation of tracks and the removal of old ones.

Originating from 1942, long range boards were introduced to centre operations rooms, tellers in contact with neighbouring groups could hand over incoming and outgoing tracks which were plotted on this map.

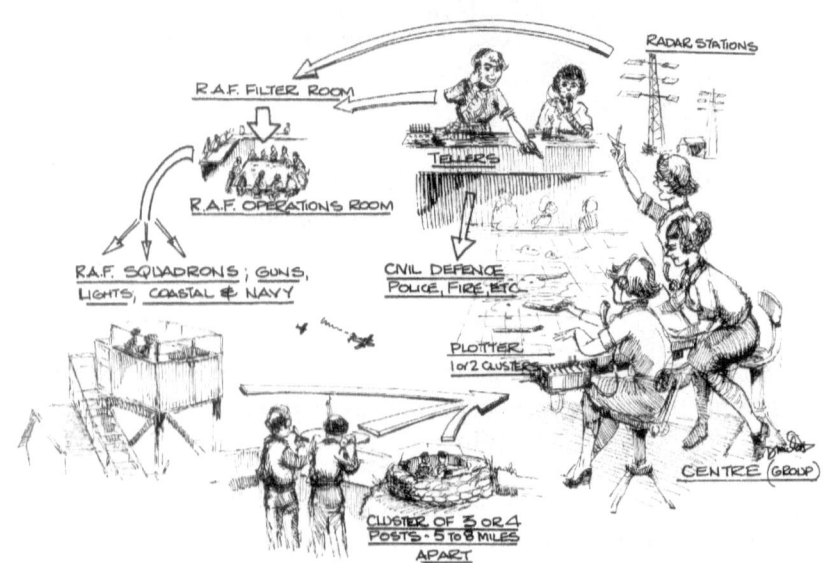

Source: ROC Journal

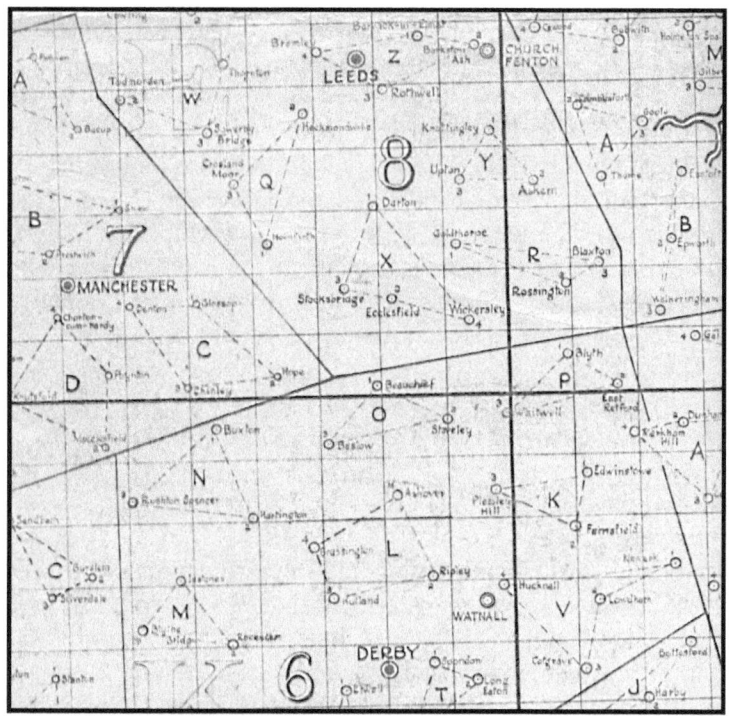

Extract of a map showing the locations of WW2 observer posts and communication links
(Source: Charles Parker)

Operations Room (Centre)

Duties in the operations room included:

- Plotters working on the plotting table and on the long range board;
- Tellers communicating with neighbouring ROC groups, fighter operations rooms, anti-aircraft and searchlight units;
- Alarm controllers in contact with the police, national alert system, Ministry of Home Security and with local factories;
- An interrogator liaising with the ground controlled interception (GCI) radar units; and

- Duty Controller, his assistant and a post controller who supervised the plotters and posts.

Obviously it was essential that observers could correctly identify an aeroplane. In 1939 aircraft recognition was not yet the highly prized skill it was to become in the Observer Corps. The other services felt that accurate identification was impossible. Observers realised that this was a deficiency and pushed to overcome the weakness through training and the use of aircraft identification literature consisting of aircraft silhouettes and data.

The War Years – "From WW2 into the Cold"

Nuclear Role

When the dust had settled in 1945 the incredible pace of development of fighting weaponry, had given, only too well, the clues to the future. On the allied side, the Atom bomb had given them a weapon which had ensured the surrender of Japan; the Germans had developed the V2 rocket which was mobile and able to be fired from any site, and for which the allies were almost powerless. The ROC continued to monitor the skies after the cessation of hostilities, and was keen to develop new ways to;

- Keep accurate tracks of potentially hostile aircraft.
- Speed up reporting to control centres.
- Handover information between neighbouring posts.

In September 1947, over a year after VE Day, the ROC held its first small scale exercise in southern England, which included for the first time substantial numbers of jet aircraft. Another year later the first large scale exercise took place; in the last two of its four days of this radar only was used.

By the end of the 1940's the Commander-in-Chief of the RAF's Fighter Command, Air Marshall Sir Basil Embry, realised the fragile nature of UK air defences with reaction times of defences being based on the wartime communication structure[20] and was deemed to be too slow to respond to the growing threat from the expansion of Soviet Forces and air power and especially in response to their related developments in nuclear weapons. Embry concluded that there wasn't deemed to be a need for Group Operations Rooms with operations being controlled more effectively through Sector Commanders. These concerns by Embry eventually culminated in the development of the "Rotor Plan".

This plan involved;

1. The transfer of RAF sector operations centres and GCI[21] radar staff into new purpose built underground bunkers which were deemed safe from conventional and most of the nuclear weapons at the time.
2. The extension of the Control and Reporting organisation using the latest early warning equipment and therefore to provide cover up the east coast to Aberdeen; down the west coast and eastwards to Portland Bill.
3. 16 Chain Home radar stations were to be overhauled to provide significant cover within the radar network.

Overground Monitoring Posts

At the same time as the Rotor Plan was being developed; the ROC was finding that aircraft monitoring was becoming increasingly difficult with the development of new faster aircraft. Even so, new aircraft Monitoring Posts were developed to assist observers to monitor aircraft. The idea for these new posts originated in 1947, however it was only during 1951/52 as part of the programme to update the air defences through the Rotor Plan that more substantial buildings were built to offer at least some level of protection from the elements or attack.

---

[20]This communication structure was from Group Control to Sector Control to RAF Station.
[21]Ground-Controlled Interception (GCI) is an air defence tactic whereby one or more radar stations are linked to a command-communications centre which guides interceptor aircraft to an airborne target.

Although some of these new structures were built of brick; many sites received pre-cast concrete panelled structures known as "Orlit" Posts, after the manufacturers of the structures Messrs Orlit Ltd. These Orlit structures were split into two sections, the entrance door led into the smaller roofed section which was used as a shelter and store with a sliding door into the open section which housed the post instrument and chart on top of a wooden mounting. Two types of Orlit posts existed; the Orlit 'A' was at ground level and the Orlit 'B' was raised on four 6'0" legs with a ladder for access.

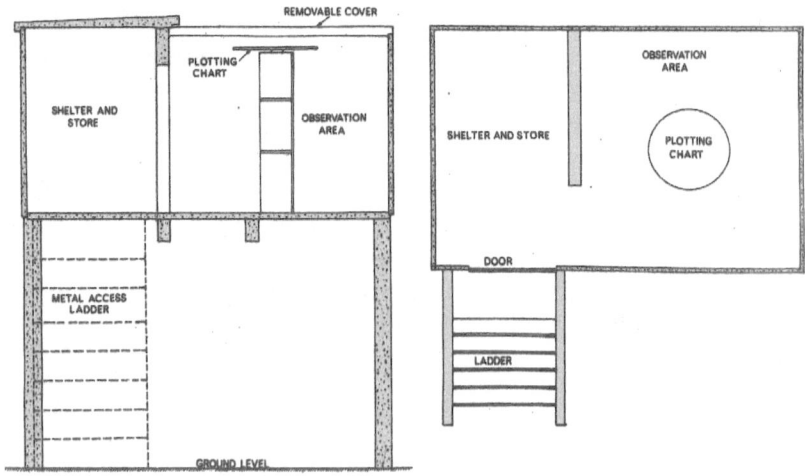

Plan of ROC Overground "Orlit B" Post. The "Orlit A" post was of a similar construction except it was not raised above the ground.
(Source: Wood, D.: Attack Warning Red – 1976)

Surviving WW2 era Orlit "A" at Burgh-on-Bain
(Source: Noel J Ryan)

Surviving WW2 era Orlit "A" at Elloughton.
(Source: Noel J Ryan)

Surviving WW2 era Orlit "B" at Holme on Spalding Moor
(Source: Noel J Ryan)

Surviving WW2 era Orlit "B" at Swallow.
(Source: Noel J Ryan)

Initial Corps' Structure during the early Cold War period

The new Rotor Plan involved the change in RAF operational sector areas which provided the opportunity for the ROC to reconfigure its own sectors to match more closely those sectors of the RAF and providing more operational effectiveness for both organisations.

The reorganisation of the ROC sector areas was scheduled for completion by 1st November 1953. The Groups were reorganised with the numbers being reduced from 40 to 31, and with the Corps now covering Northern Ireland for the first time. As a result of the reorganisation the groups covering Yorkshire were reduced from 3 to 2.

The former 9 and 10 groups merged to form 20 Group centred on York with the area of control changing to encompass an area between the northern South Yorkshire boundary and northern North Yorkshire boundary. The Group Control for the South Yorkshire area was still located in Leeds (within the 20 Group area of control) at Grove House (until 1964) however the Leeds 8 Group was renumbered to 18 Group and the area of control now encompassing the areas of the East Riding of Yorkshire and Hull formerly under the control of 10 Group.

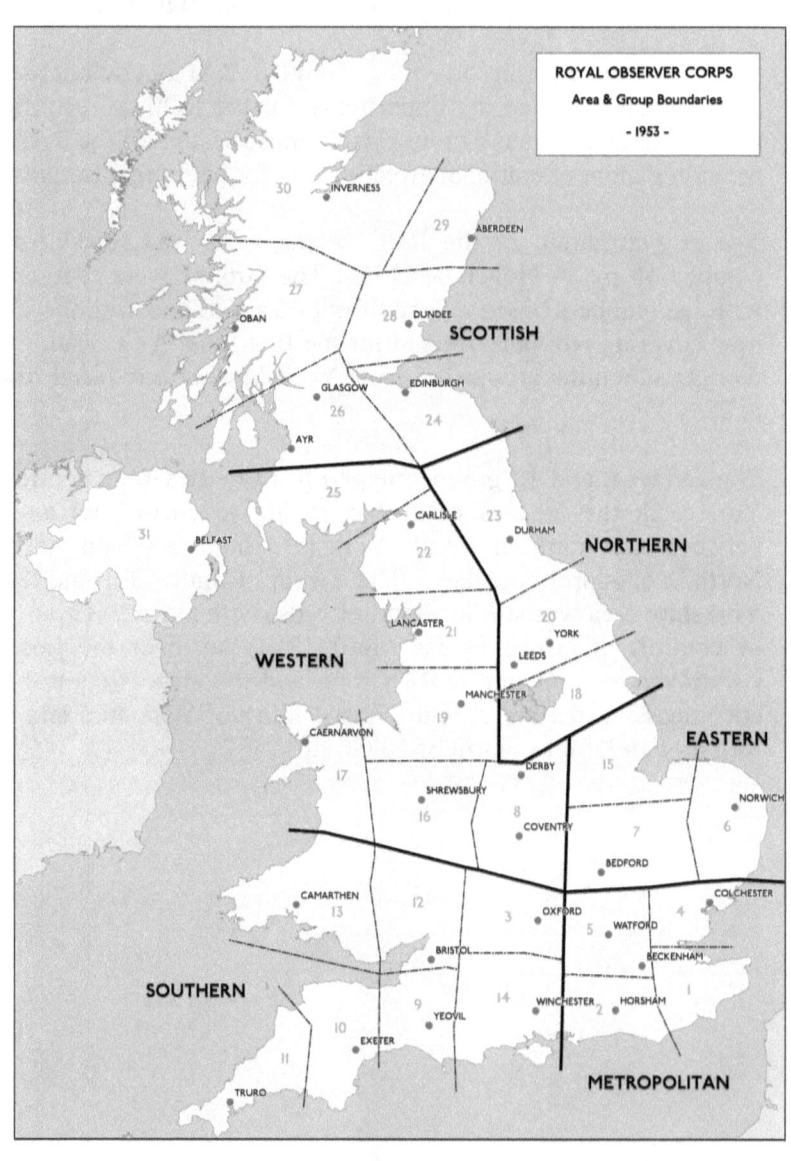

Royal Observer Corps Sectors & Groups in 1953
Source: SYROCM

Another role for the ROC in the defence against nuclear weapons was announced in the House of Commons on the 15th June 1955:-

"... Steps are being taken for the ROC to give warning of and to measure radioactivity in the event of air attacks in a future war."

The ROC was given the task of reporting any nuclear bomb bursts and monitoring the resultant radioactive fall-out. The ROC was obviously suited to this new role; the infrastructure and lines of communication were already in place and the personnel involved were familiar with the monitoring equipment.

The first significant exercise involving the ROC in handling nuclear data was in 1956. The aircraft spotting and identification responsibilities of the ROC diminished during the 1950s and were replaced by the need for nuclear warning and monitoring.

UKWMO

In 1957 the British government's policy of reliance on nuclear weapons became clear. Within ten years the aircraft recognition and reporting role of the ROC had all but gone. Later in 1957 the United Kingdom Warning and Monitoring Organisation (UKWMO) was set up under Home Office control and funding, with five main functions;

1. Warning the public of any air attack – conventional or nuclear.
2. Providing confirmation of nuclear strike.
3. Warning the public of the approach of radioactive fallout.
4. Provision of a post-attack meteorological service for fallout prediction.
5. Supplying the civilian and military authorities in the United Kingdom and neighbouring countries in NATO with details of nuclear bursts and with a scientific assessment of the path and intensity of fallout

The United Kingdom was divided initially into six, UK Warning and Monitoring Sectors, based upon the current ROC Group and Sector structure as from November 1953. It was intended that

UKWMO would provide civil and military authorities in Britain with information during a nuclear attack. The ROC would provide the first data on the positions and extent of the attack. This data would be used by UKWMO, in conjunction with weather information from the Meteorological Office, to produce a forecast of radioactive fallout. As this fallout occurred, its strength and position would be mapped using data from posts, enabling further fallout forecasts to be given.

"Going Underground"

The added responsibility of reporting nuclear bursts and monitoring fallout and the minimal level of protection from a nuclear bomb meant that such tasks could not be achieved within the current overground Monitoring Posts. These posts were simply not set up to provide any degree of protection from a nuclear explosion.

After the successful trial of the building of an underground post at Farnham, Surrey in 1956 a network of underground posts were planned to be constructed over the next 3 to 4 years. The locations of these underground posts were usually adjacent to existing posts although some had to be sited some distance away in order to provide effective underground monitoring capabilities. The underground posts were constructed with concrete under a 200 mm slab; they were 4.75 metres long and 2.25 metres in length and height with power being supplied from 12 volt batteries inside the post and a petrol generator used to charge the batteries sited outside the post (see chapter 9).

It was necessary for these posts (as well as centres) to be occupied for at least seven days and possibly even up to two weeks or greater after any nuclear event depending upon the situation. Conditions in these posts were cramped and cold and in some damp; although many of these worst ones were abandoned (e.g. Thorne), and it was fortunate for observers that long occupation was never necessary, in practise. Later posts were insulated with polystyrene tiles on walls and ceiling and had rubber matting cut from National Coal Board underground conveyor belts on the floors to provide insulation from the cold.

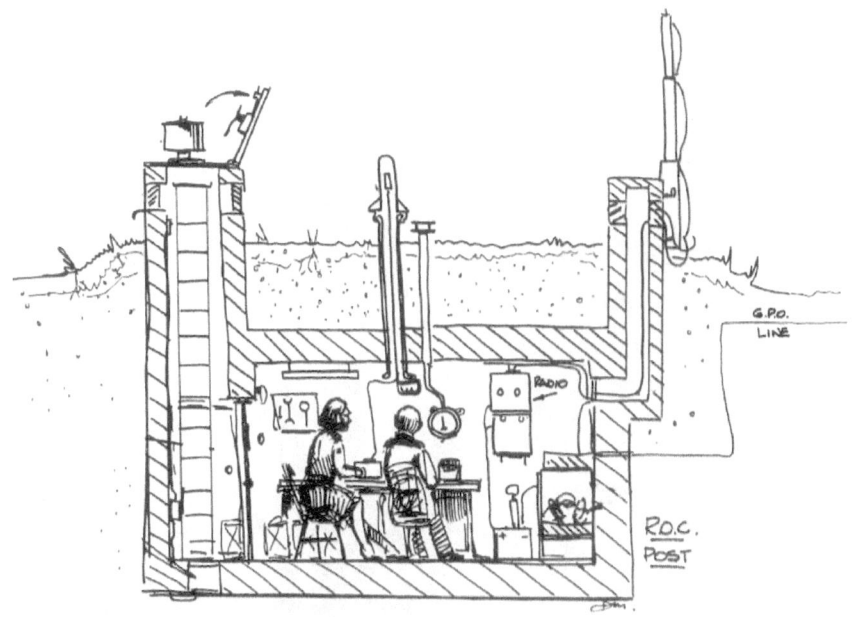
ROC Underground Monitoring Post

Altogether more sophisticated than its earlier role; the ROC formed part of the United Kingdom Warning and Monitoring Organisation (UKWMO) which was the only organisation in Britain equipped and trained to report on radioactive fallout on a national basis. The fact that the Corps was trained to obtain and disseminate this information might have well meant the difference between life and death for many of us.

Group Controls

At roughly the same time as the underground Monitoring Posts were being built, a number of protected Group Control Headquarters were being developed. Although initially planned in 1956, development didn't commence until 1959 with the majority of sites becoming operational in 1960/61. These controls collated all information from the Monitoring Posts within their group and aimed to establish the exact location, height and power of the nuclear explosion. In total 31 Group Controls were constructed and ranged in design from either semi-sunk (12); surface (13) or existing buildings (6).

Nuclear fallout monitoring within ROC Group Control

Further Reorganisation

Economic constraints during the mid to late 1960s led to reduced defence spending by the UK Government and ultimately led to a need to reduce defence spending by the Government. As part of the Government's Home Defence review during 1968, the Government decided to reduce home defence (civil defence) to a care and maintenance basis and disband the Civil Defence Corps, Auxiliary Fire Service and the Territorial and Army Volunteer Reserve (Category III).

Concerns by ROC members in respect to these defence cuts ultimately led to the issue of a letter for communication to all ROC members by Observer Captain W. Rusby on 17th January 1968. The letter highlighted that;

"The Warning and Monitoring Organisation and therefore the ROC was not included in the "Civil Defence" decision and is to continue in being, but is subjected to a severe financial cut that will

> *impose the need for reappraisal of tasks for the Corps and organisation required to meet the reduced requirements ... it is clear (however) that a scaling down of activity will be inevitable".*

As a result of this scaling down of the ROC activity it was decided that the number of underground monitoring posts throughout Great Britain & Northern Ireland would be reduced from 1559 to 873 from 1st April 1968. At the same time a sector and group reorganisation led to the Group Headquarters at Watford (No.5 Group) and Leeds (No.18 Group) being disbanded and staffing reduced by half to approximately 324 spare-time officers and 12,300 observers.

The reorganisation of the sectors in 1968 reduced the total number from 6 to 5. Each of these sectors had five UKWMO Groups within them and each group had an underground headquarters; with one of these being the sector control headquarters. Each group had a number of Monitoring Posts, varying between 27 and 58 and spaced between 10 and 15 miles apart. These monitoring posts reported directly to the Group control. Between 1960 and 1991, South Yorkshire's underground Posts were under the control of four Group controls; all within the Midland region.

GROUP NO.	HQ LOCATION	BUILDING TYPE
From 1964 to 1968		
18	Leeds (Yeadon)	Semi-sunk
From 1968 to 1991		
8	Coventry (Rugby)	Semi-sunk
15	Lincoln	Semi-sunk
20	York	Semi-sunk

The table below lists the main five sectors and respective group headquarters as from 1968. Sector-Group HQ's are shown in bold.

SECTOR	GROUP NO.	HQ LOCATION
Metropolitan	1	Maidstone
	2	**HORSHAM**
	3	Oxford
	4	Colchester
	14	Winchester
Midland	6	Norwich
	7	Bedford
	8	Coventry (Rugby)
	15	**LINCOLN**
	20	York
Southern	9	Yeovil
	10	Exeter
	12	**BRISTOL**
	13	South Wales (Carmarthen)
	16	Shrewsbury
Western	17	North Wales (Wrexham)
	21	**PRESTON**
	22	Carlisle
	23	Durham
	31	Belfast
Caledonian	24	Edinburgh
	25	Ayr
	28	**DUNDEE**
	29	Aberdeen
	30	Inverness

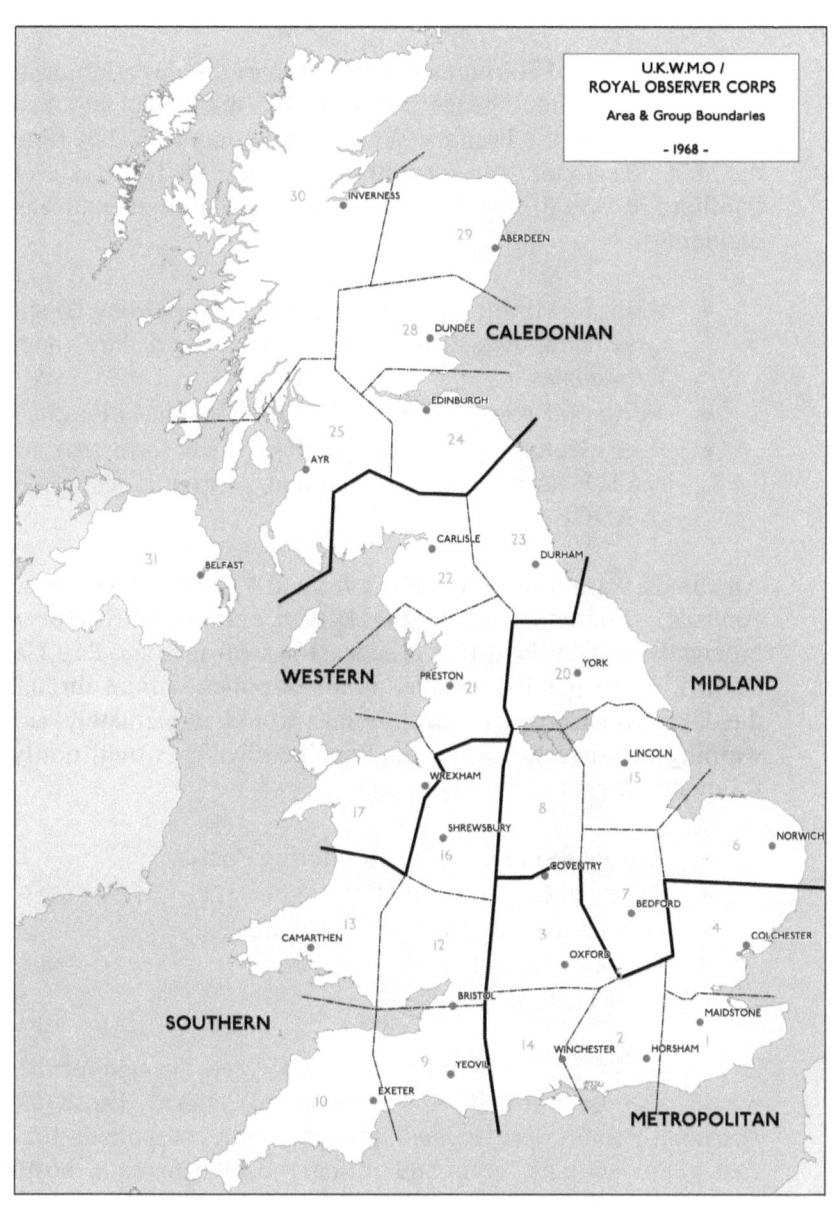

UKWMO Sectors & Groups from 1968
Source: SYROCM

Air Attack Warning System

The origination of warnings to the public of the threat of air attack was based on intelligence received by the Principal Warning Officer based at the Primary War Headquarters (PWHQ) formerly the UK Regional Air Operations Centre (UKRAOC). Such intelligence would have been gathered from a number of sources including;

- Ballistic Missile Early Warning System (BMEWS) sites in Greenland, Alaska and on the North Yorkshire moors at Fylingdales.
- Northern Radar System (NORAD) based in Colorado, US.
- RAF Sector Operations Centres which form part of the NATO Air defence Ground Environment System (NADGE).

Air attack warnings were passed from PWHQ (or selected sector controls) simultaneously to the BBC Central Control for radio broadcast; and by land-line broadcast system to some 250 Carrier Control Points (CCPs) installed in major police stations throughout the UK. The Carrier Control Points would immediately issue a warning message to all Carrier Receivers which would notify the following groups of imminent attack;

- Royal Observer Corps Monitoring Posts.
- Regional Government HQs
- Local Authority Emergency Centres,
- Home Defence Forces
- Nuclear Reporting Cells

A network of 19,000 Warning Points located throughout the UK would also be notified of the imminent attack. These 19,000 Warning Points were located predominantly at police, fire and coastguard stations, civil and military establishments, hospitals, rural areas and various industrial centres.

Remote Controlled Power Operated Siren located on the chimney of the former Ecclesfield Police Station, Sheffield
(Source: S W Craine)

Of these sites, 9,000 were equipped with hand operated sirens and maroons, 2000 with sirens only and 3,000 with fallout warning maroons[22] only. The remaining 5,000 were receiver points. Simultaneously by remote control, all power operated sirens would be activated to provide the Warning Attack. The following types of warning would be given to the public:

---

[22] Fallout Warning Maroons were devices which were fired into the sky and produced three loud bangs to signify the approach of nuclear fallout. Further details of these instruments will be described in a later chapter.

Attack Warning - RED

Meaning: Imminent danger from air attack.
Signal: Given by power or hand-operated sirens and consisting of a rising and falling note for approximately one-minute; and by BBC broadcast.

All Clear - WHITE

Meaning: No further risk of attack or fallout.
Signal: Given by power or hand-operated siren and consisting of a steady note for approximately one minute.

These warnings were a direct follow-on from air attack during WW2. With the added threat from nuclear fallout from 1957 a further warning was developed:-

Fallout Warning - BLACK

Meaning: Imminent danger of radioactive fallout.
Signal: Given by maroon, gongs or whistle (three bangs or blasts in quick succession), and by BBC broadcast.

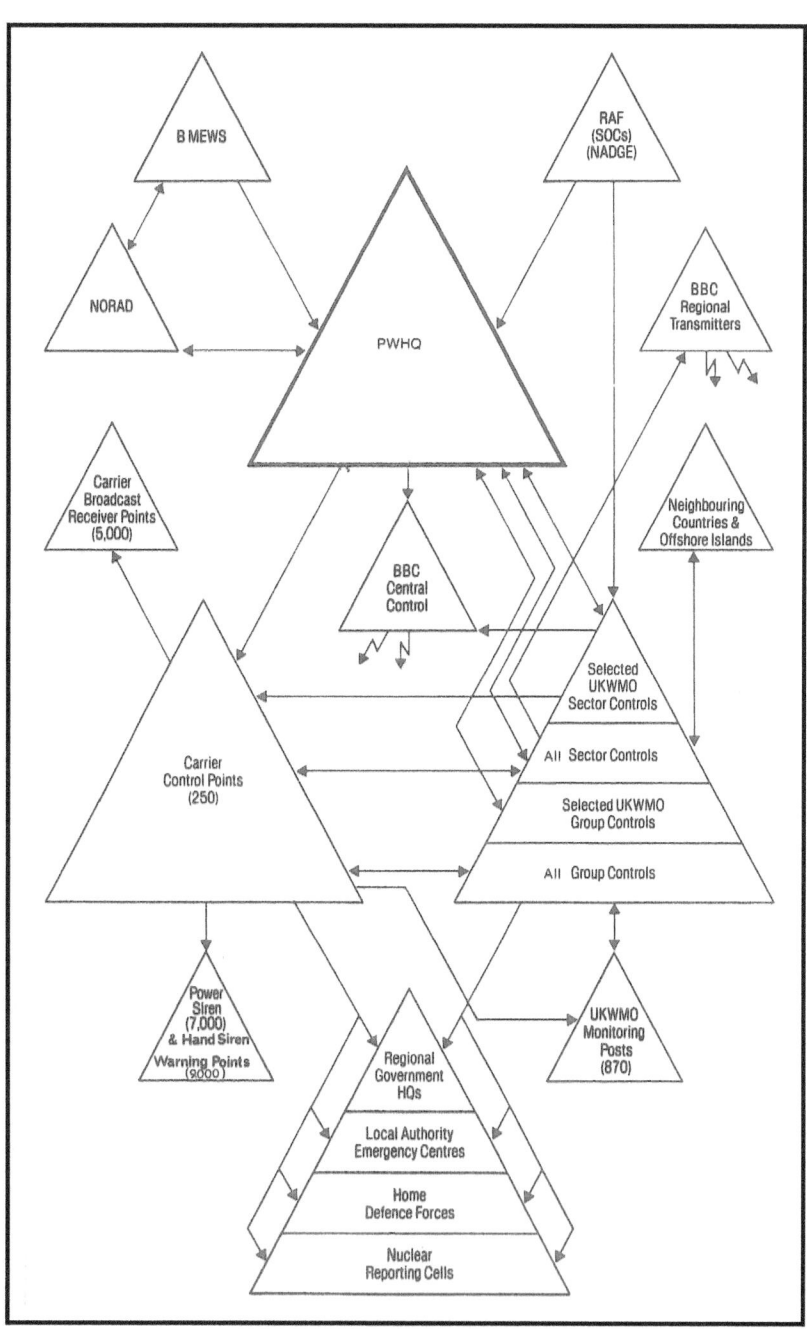

Air Attack Warning System
Source: ROC Training Manual

"Over-Ground"

Thanks to the array of instruments and apparatus embodied in the 25 (post-1968) reinforced Group Controls and the underground Monitoring Posts, the Corps would have been able to supply essential data on the arrival and intensity of the fallout. This would enable officers of the United Kingdom Warning and Monitoring Organisation at group controls, to advise people in the path of radioactive dust to take cover or to advise the armed forces or other controlling authorities which areas are safe for access and operations by land, air or sea. Fallout warnings (BLACK) would be passed over the carrier system to the numerous Carrier Control Points and thence onto the warning points within the carrier area.

The ROC was ideally suited for its role of reporting fallout. The strategically placed network extended from the Orkneys to the far south-west. Although the role of the Corps had changed completely during the 1960s and 70s, the traditional links with the Royal Air Force remained and the skill of visual aircraft recognition was still maintained by post observers up until stand-down in 1991.

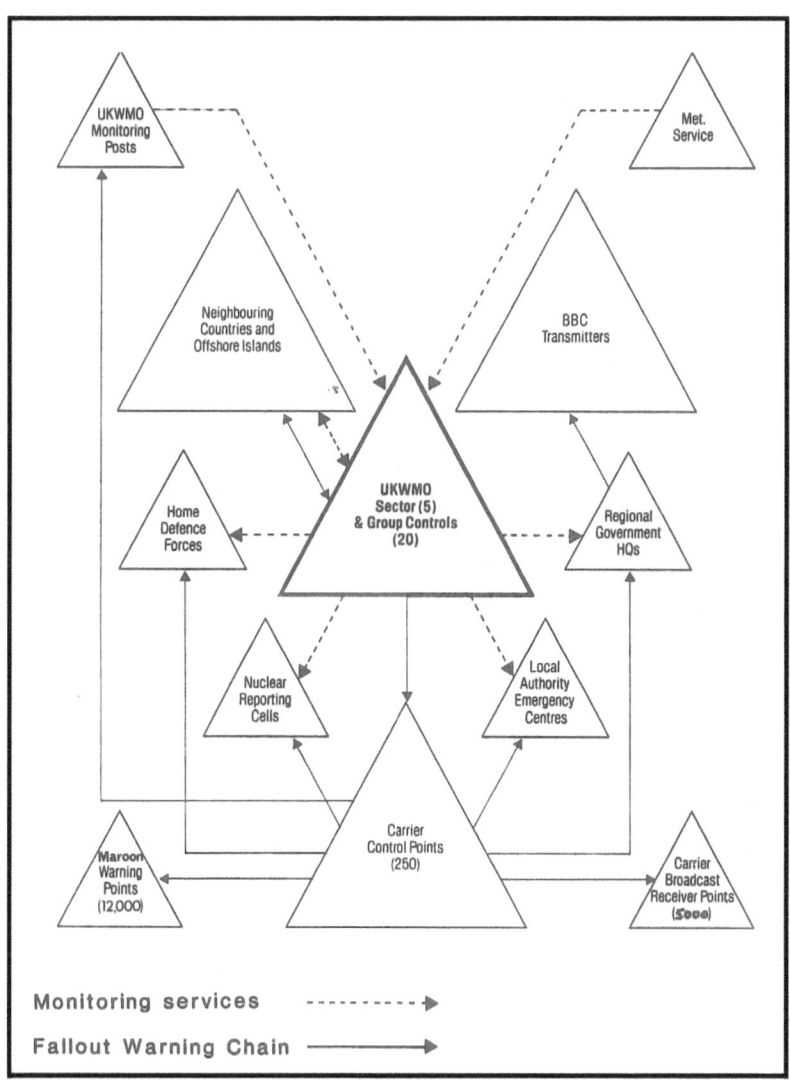

UK Fallout Warning System
Source: ROC Training Manual

"AWDREY"

AWDREY (Atomic Weapons Detection Recognition and Estimation of Yield) was designed, built and maintained by the Atomic Weapons Establishment at Aldermaston. The system was designed to detect the blast of a nuclear explosion through the registering of the initial and subsequent intense flash generated by the explosion either by the electro-magnetic pulse that the explosion generates or from the flash generated by the blast. From these effects, an estimate the nuclear devices power (yield) could be determined.

The units were not located at all Group Controls, but were located far enough apart that a simultaneous response on two AWDREY units could only be registered as a nuclear explosion and not be triggered from a lightning strike which would generally affect only one AWDREY. A further machine called DIADEM (Direction Indicator of Atomic Detonation by Electronic Means) worked with AWDREY and enabled the identification of the likely bearing of the explosion.

ROC post bomb detection instruments such as the Bomb Power Indicator (BPI) operated by recording the pressure of the blast wave from any nearby nuclear explosion. Any ultra-high-altitude nuclear explosion, designed to knock out the UK's communications and electronic equipment would not produce a detectable blast wave and the AWDREY system was therefore the only method of identifying these bursts.

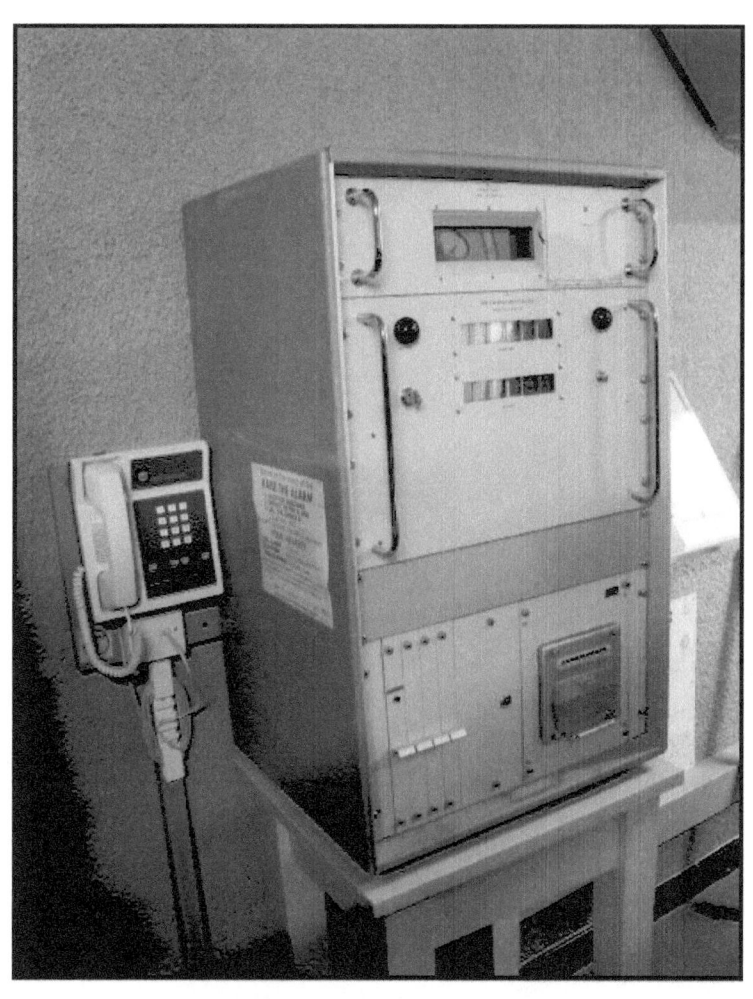

AWDREY Unit at York ROC Group Control
(Source: Chris Howells Collection)
[www.chrishowells.co.uk]

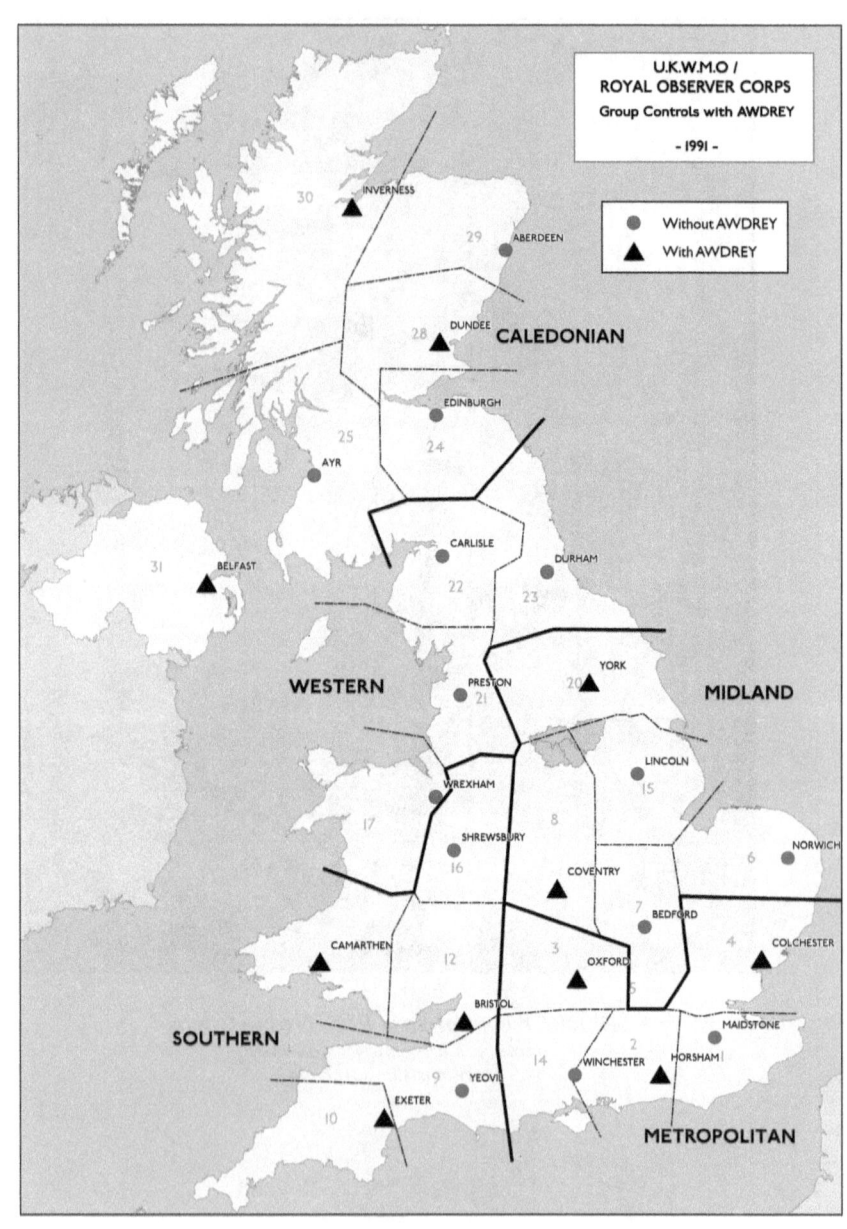

ROC Group Controls with AWDREY unit
(Source: SYROCM)

Nuclear Reporting Cells – "The Secret Corps"

During the 1970s and as a development of the Special Nuclear Operations Teams created in 1958 at RAF Bentley Priory, a new class of observer was created to operate specialist Nuclear Reporting Cells (NRC). These NRC's were located at selected strategic armed forces Headquarters across the country.

The initial role of the NRC observers was to provide the army, navy and air force with comprehensive visual displays and scientific interpretation of the information provided by the ROC group controls with respect to nuclear bomb bursts and radioactive fallout dispersal. Their role combined basic ROC training (as other Monitoring Posts and group control staff) and duties with some of the scientific skills and training of the Home Office warning teams. Higher levels of security clearance and specialist training were needed for the limited number of NRC observers as a result.

The NRCs post 1991 - "Beyond the Cold"

While the main body of the Royal Observer Corps was stood down from operational service a decision was taken by the Ministry of Defence (MOD) to retain the Nuclear Reporting Cell (NRC) element of the Corps, in order to continue providing a Nuclear, Biological and Chemical (NBC) service for all three armed forces.

From October 1991 17 (later reduced to 16) NRCs were retained and staffed by 240 other ranks and 16 spare-time officers with control of the NRC groups being transferred from the UKWMO to the administration of Headquarters ROC (HQROC) based at RAF Bentley Priory. At the same time the name of the NRC's changed to Nuclear, Biological and Chemical Cell (NBCC) to reflect their main role of the provision of Nuclear, Biological and Chemical Assessments for the military forces. The control of the Corps had therefore gone full circle; the Corps was once again fully funded and controlled by the Royal Air Force and became part of Headquarters No 11 Group at RAF Bentley Priory.

HQROC, which comprised two whole-time officers and two MOD civilian staff, continued to administrate the remaining NBC cells which were now based at various RAF / military installations throughout the UK. Operations within the Cells were based on the NATO NBC procedures (ATP45) which generally consisted of;

- Prediction of chemical hazard areas and meteorological considerations
- The estimation of the yield of a nuclear device
- The prediction of nuclear fallout onshore and at sea
- General Information relating to the nature and importance of nuclear fallout

From 1991 the ever diminishing threat to the UK continued with the ROC staff providing a high level of service to their clients within the Cells. At the same time however many believed there to exist power struggles within the RAF / RAF Regiment and especially in the senior elements of the RAF Regiment who felt that it was not right that spare time civilians undertook the NBC role, when cuts to full-time servicemen was a possibility. Ultimately the decision was finally taken to stand-down the remaining element of the Royal Observer Corps on the 31st December 1995.

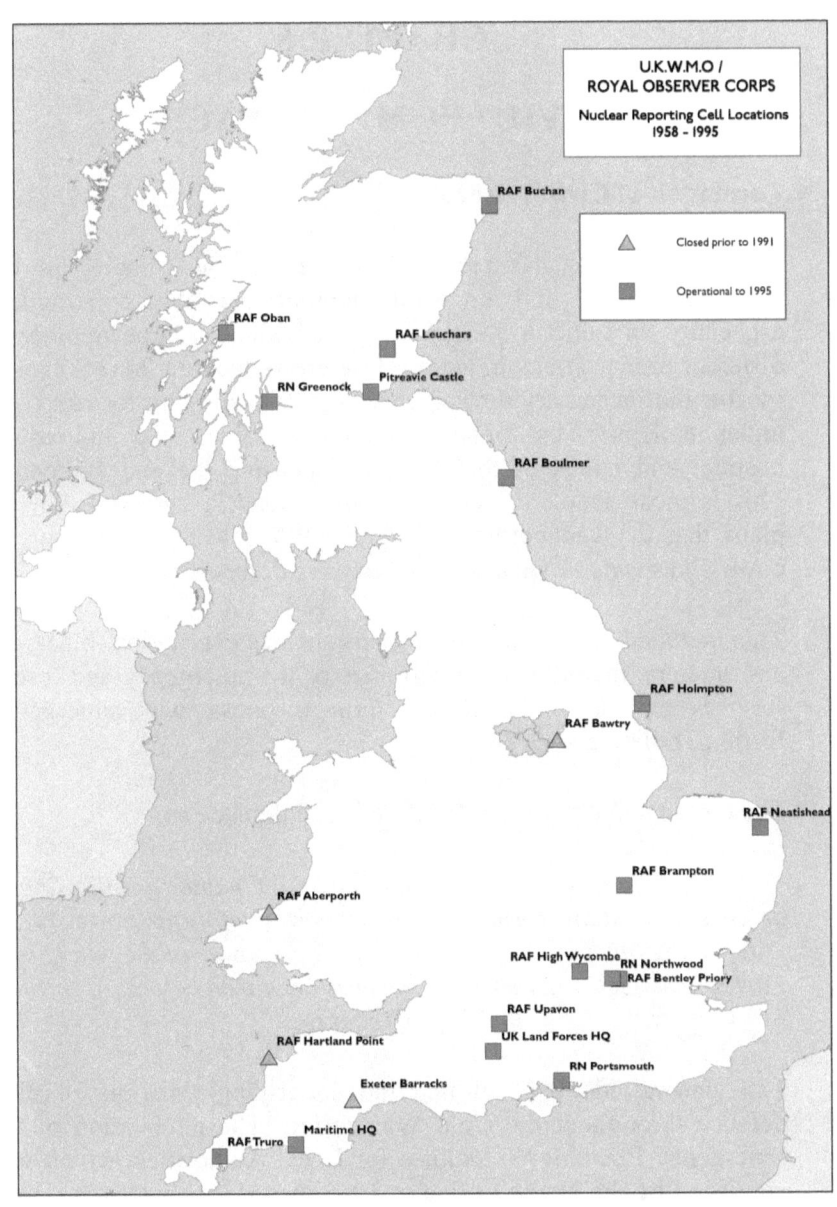

ROC Nuclear Reporting Cells - 1958 to 1995
(Source: Lawrence Holmes)

CHAPTER 5

CIVIL / HOME DEFENCE

Formation of Civil Defence

The many films and recorded images of the attacks on the industrial towns and cities throughout the United Kingdom especially on London during the "Blitz" show a large number of different organisations in action. Fire crews tackling blazes caused by fire and incendiary devices; rescue parties digging for survivors under collapsed buildings; ambulances taking the injured to hospital and ladies of the WRVS dispensing tea and sympathy. This is most people's idea of "Civil Defence"; but civil defence plans that evolved before and during WW2 went beyond this to cover all aspects of what is called passive defence.

This included pre-attack preparations such as evacuation, black out and shelters, then the wider activities of the emergency and rescue services and later the longer term response with emergency feeding, billeting and rebuilding.

The Civil Defence Act 1948 defined civil defence as;

"...any measure not amounting to actual combat for affording defence against any form of hostile attack by a foreign power or for depriving any form of attack by a foreign power of the whole or part of its effect, whether the measures are taken before, at or after the time of the attack".

This general ideology formed the underlying principle of civil defence throughout the Cold War period. The publication of the Emergency Planning Guidelines for Local Authorities, which was published by the Home Office in 1985, based its objectives on the principles laid down by the Civil Defence Act.

It thereby promoted the need for civil defence to:-

- provide protection against the immediate effects of conventional and nuclear weapons;
- ensure the maximum use of the precautions that could save large numbers of people from the effects of radiation;
- plan to meet shortages in food, accommodation and avoid disruption which would follow war;
- plan for the restoration of essential supplies and services and
- set the groundwork and organisation that would help promote recovery.

In many cases these principles were valid. However, initial protection to the population in the form of nuclear shelters was limited due to cost and resource constraints. It was deemed uneconomic to provide funding for a full network of nuclear shelters to protect the total population from nuclear attack.

A greater need was seen for the preservation of the basic institutions of the state and hence to provide the continuation of Government during and after a nuclear war and it was therefore with this in mind that the majority of protective shelters were provided and developed during the cold war.

The principle for the protection of the population was however not ignored and formed the production of a number of key publications aimed to reassure and assist the population to protect themselves if the worst happened.

Selection of "Civil Protection" booklets issued from 1950s to Present
(Source: S W Craine)

By the late 1960s the key objective of civil defence was to maintain the machinery of government at all levels (local, regional to national) as to increase the prospects of and to direct national survival and recovery in the post-attack period.

Civil Defence Corps

The introduction of the Civil Defence (Public Protection) Regulations in 1949 gave all county and borough councils responsibility prior to, during and after a nuclear attack for:-

- collecting and distributing intelligence about the attack;
- controlling and co-ordinating action necessary as a result of the attack;
- rescue;
- protection against "the toxic effects of atomic, biological and chemical warfare" and

- advising the public on the effects of attack and protective measures to take.

Local authorities would also have to:-

- organise evacuation and reception
- provide care of the homeless
- provide information centres
- identify and dispose of any dead
- provide emergency water and food supplies

More importantly however the local authorities would have to organise and develop a new Civil Defence Corps organisation within their area that was to form the key element in civil defence plans.

It was initially suggested that the Civil Defence Corps should be a branch of the armed forces and to be organised on similar lines to the army reserves however instead; the corps was established as a civilian voluntary body administered by local authorities in a similar form as the previous Air Raid Precautions organisation during WW2.

The aim of the corps was to assist local authorities to comply with the newly imposed civil defence functions and was to consist of divisions of unpaid but uniformed volunteers enrolled by "Corps Authorities" i.e. the County Councils and County Borough Councils and organised by them. The overall policy and conditions for the corps were to be determined by the Home Secretary who announced them in a series of civil defence circulars (or CDCs) to the Authorities.

Recruiting for the Corps, and related organisations; including the Auxiliary Fire Service (AFS) and National Hospital Reserve Service, started in late 1949 with training being undertaken by qualified instructors; most of whom had been to one of the civil defence schools that were set up in 1956 at Falfield, Easingwold and Tayworth Castle, who undertook to train the body of Corps members in areas such as:-

- Principles of Rescue
- First Aid
- Fire Fighting
- Radiation Assessment and Analysis

The Organisation of the Civil Defence Corps

For operational purposes, the local divisions provided by the corps authorities would join together into areas and then groups. The group controller would work under the direction of the regional commissioner at the regional war room. Each of the approximately 400 groups and areas in England and Wales including approximately 70 in Scotland would require its own control centre.

The Home Office had given some suggestions about setting up these centres in the early 1950s. These reflected practices from WW2. Centres were to be set up on the size of the local population and would normally be sited away from potential targets such as railway yards and factory complexes. Their role would be:-

"...a communications and intelligence centre at which the controller and his staff will operate during the mobilisation and life saving periods, and if necessary into the survival period".

They would not be used continually and would not need anything other than basic domestic facilities. Whilst many authorities re-used WW2 centres and many new ones were opened a large number of authorities lacked effective control premises. The Civil Defence Corps were divided into operational sections to reflect their role in responding to the immediate effects of a nuclear attack at local level.

SECTION	ROLE
HEADQUARTERS	• Provide and operate static and mobile controls at the various local levels of the control chain, • To provide communications, undertake reconnaissance and provide scientific advice to Controllers.
WARDEN	• To provide a link between the individual and mobile services. • In a nuclear war he would become the leader of his neighbourhood, advising and controlling the public and seeing that the survivors get help and attention. • Responsible for local reconnaissance and reporting, for the organisation of street parties and the deployment of life-saving services within their areas. • Responsibilities in connection with warnings of radioactive fallout and control of the public in areas affected by it.
WELFARE	• Dispersal of priority classes • Provide immediate help with food and shelter and in the longer term with organising community life. • The location and arrangement of accommodation for any homeless survivors or refugees in rest centres • Organise emergency feeding for such survivors.

SECTION	ROLE
RESCUE	• To provide units for rescue, first aid provision, debris clearance and emergency demolition work. • To work alongside the regular fire service (and members of the volunteer based Auxiliary Fire Service who were trained in home defence fire fighting) and members of the armed forces, particularly the RAF and the emergency services.
AMBULANCE & FIRST AID	• To administer First Aid to casualties, • Organising casualty evacuation to forward medical aid units and to hospital. • In war, it would merge with the peacetime ambulance service and work alongside the health services, which would be augmented by the National Hospital Service Reserve. The NHRS would provide qualified nurses and nursing auxiliaries for the expanded hospital service.

The Roles of the Civil Defence Corps

CDC Mobile Columns

The early 1950s saw the Home Office set up a Mobile Civil Defence Column to experiment with the idea of moving a large body of civil defence personnel and their equipment to a city after it had been hit by an atom bomb. As developments with the Hydrogen bomb progressed, then the need for Mobile Columns changed and ultimately led to the development of the Mobile Defence Corps in 1955 who were trained and equipped for all rescue, fire fighting and ambulance duties. Unlike the Civil

Defence Corps however, the Mobile group was to be staffed by military "reserve" personnel rather than volunteer civilians. The group was however reliant on the need for personnel especially those who had completed their National Service and with the lack of reservists available to fill the numbers for the Mobile Columns and with the proposed ending of National Service[23] in 1960 the mobile corps were disbanded in 1957.

> *Mobile Defence Corps (Disbandment)*
> HANSARD 03 December 1958 vol 596 cc141-2W
>
> **Mr. Gresham Cooke:** *asked the Secretary of State for War whether, in view of the contemplated end of National Service, he will make a statement about the future of the Mobile Defence Corps.*
>
> **Mr. Soames:** *The Mobile Defence Corps was formed in 1955 as a mobile force trained in Civil Defence techniques to support local Civil Defence organisations and link the civil and military efforts in this field. Most of its members were National Service men in the reserve forces. With the end of part-time training of National Service men, and the prospective end of National Service itself, it has become clear that a Mobile Defence Corps consisting solely of volunteers will not be able to carry out its tasks. In these circumstances I have decided, with regret, that I should advise the Queen that the Corps should be disbanded at the end of February, 1959. To give the essential assistance to Civil Defence, artillery and infantry units of the T.A. will be given advanced training in Civil Defence techniques. One year's camp in every four starting next year will be set aside for the purpose. These duties will be additional to the present fighting role of the T.A. units concerned. They will not replace it and will not alter any unit's organisation. I know the House will join with me in paying tribute to the volunteer members of the Mobile Defence Corps. The methods which they have developed will be of great value to the T.A. units which take up the task. They have also engendered a spirit of close co-operation between the Army and Civil Defence authorities and this will be maintained and fostered under the new arrangements.*

Auxiliary Fire Service (AFS)[24]

The Auxiliary Fire Service (AFS) was initially formed in 1938 as part of Civil Defence Air Raid Precautions, which led to the creation of an AFS group in every county borough, borough and

---

[23] National Service as peacetime conscription was formalised by the National Service Act 1948. From 1 January 1949, every healthy man between 17 and 21 was expected to serve in the armed forces for 18 months, and remain on the reserve list for four years, with a liability to be recalled to their units for up to twenty days service or training on not more than three occasions in the four years.

[24] Information provided by the kind permission for use by Mark Johnson.

urban district area. Each AFS was commanded by a Commandant, with Deputy and/or Assistant Commandants in the larger services. The services operated their own fire stations, each commanded by a section officer, and station areas were divided into fire beats, each under the command of a patrol officer. Services with five or more stations divided them into divisions, each under the command of a divisional officer. These ranks were not laid down by the government, and some services used different systems.

The role of the AFS was to supplement the work of local fire brigades by offering fire fighting assistance from the groups of part-time and unpaid volunteers within their respective service areas. The WW2 AFS role was however severely hampered by the incompatibility of equipment used by the different borough and county brigades - most importantly the lack of a standard size of hydrant valve. As a result, in August 1941 it was decided to create a combined brigade; the National Fire Service consisting of the AFS with the regional brigades.

Preparing for War

Under the Civil Defence Act 1948, the Auxiliary Fire Service was reformed alongside the Civil Defence Corps and gradually started to be equipped with a range of equipment ranging from light portable pumps to vehicles such as the Land Rover, Austin Gypsy and especially Bedford fire appliances commonly known as "Green Goddesses" and which were developed as water pumpers configured with high capacity pumps for high rates of pumping requirements.

Recruitment

Recruitment to the AFS began immediately and fire authorities were expected to arrange for the creation and administration of recruiting centres and enrolment. The organisation was to be based on existing fire stations and no new construction could be approved at that time. The training syllabus involved a 60-hour course.

The minimum age was 30 years but no upper age limit had been set. The aim was to enrol two male auxiliary firemen for every full time fireman and one auxiliary fireman for every part-time fireman. Later experience did in fact indicate that it would probably be necessary for some AFS members to become whole time members. Recruitment was a task that, from the beginning, was reported by all Chief Fire Officers as being difficult and various campaigns or publicity events only managed to produce limited results, with efforts to increase numbers in any given year often being balanced by those who left the organisation.

Civil defence training was also a requirement for all local authority brigade members and included:

- Civil Defence organisation
- high explosive missiles and bombs
- atomic warfare
- chemical warfare
- biological warfare and protective measures

AFS personnel were trained in firefighting by their own officers and with assistance from full-time fire officers and during peacetime, AFS crews frequently attended fires and accidents alongside their regular colleagues.

The "Green Goddess" Appliance

Initially the vehicles issued were those that remained in Government storage from WW2 and were still painted grey. Progressively, from 1953 onwards, purpose built vehicles were issued specifically designed for the AFS, all painted dark green. The pumping appliances came to be known as "Green Goddesses". In total approximately 3,100 "Green Goddess" appliances were built by Bedford Trucks then part of Vauxhall Motors and were built by a variety of bodybuilders, most of which were well known bus and coach builders at the time. Coachbuilders such as Park Royal in London, Weymann, Harringtons and Plaxtons at

Scarborough[25] all built bodies for the Green Goddesses between 1952 and 1957.

The vehicles were built in two designs:-

- The 4x2 version (based on a Bedford SB chassis and designated SHZ) was the most common type with approximately 1,300 being built. These were fitted with the 1,000 gallons per minute (gpm) pump and a 400 gallon tank.
- The 4x4 version (based on the military based Bedford RL Chassis and designated RLHZ) of which approximately 1,800 were built. These were fitted with a 900 gallons per minute (gpm) centrifugal pump and 300 gallon tank

Rather than to extinguish fires, the main role of these appliances was to pump huge quantities of water, from lakes, rivers, canals and other sources into cities hit by a nuclear attack. As such the pumping of water was generally seen as the primary role with fire fighting becoming a secondary role.

The machines could be linked together in a relay system over a number of miles, with the "Green Goddesses" forming the ability to maintain water pressure through the hose from their powerful pumps. The use of an inflatable dam assisted within the relay system and this dam was fed using several Light Portable Pumps which were fed from a suitable water source. Sometimes it was required to float these pumps directly on the water source using a specially designed 'bikini' raft.

AFS Mobile Columns

The experience of fire-fighting operations during WW2 and the need to move reinforcement convoys (columns) to cities under attack was to be the foundation of the new organisation. In May 1952 senior fire officers began attending the Fire Service College,

---

[25] Others include, Whitsons, Papworth Everard, Strachan, Willowbrook, Windover and Longwell Green Coachworks.

Dorking, to be introduced to the planned Columns and the logistics involved.

In January 1953 a Civil Defence 'Mobile Column Depot' was opened by the Home Secretary at Epsom, Surrey. It was here that 150 military personnel were seconded to work up and develop the formation of both the Civil Defence and AFS Mobile Columns. Following a period of trials and development, the AFS Mobile Column was fully established in concept and AFS personnel began training on their formation and mobilisation. Various types and numbers of vehicles were issued to brigades around the UK.

Each brigade was part of a region and each region was structured to be able to establish, on mobilisation, a number of Mobile Columns. The vehicle types would be mobilised to rendezvous points where Columns would be formed prior to operational deployment. The overall make-up of a column was designed to make it possible for it to be self sufficient in terms of fuel, feeding, accommodation and equipment / repairs. In times of war enhanced equipment such as inflatable structures would also have been issued. When mobilised in conjunction with a Civil Defence Corps Column the capabilities were vast.

Further Reorganisation

In July 1962, the Government announced plans for the re-organisation of the AFS, along with all other civil defence services.

The plans included a 'weeding out' of the now many ineffective and non participating members, the setting of a new reduced recruitment age of 17 and an upper age limit of 55 years. There were to be two categories of personnel:

- 'Fully Operational' on a 3 year engagement
- 'Fully Trained' as far as basic tests and on the Reserve thereafter

Reservists would have completed 50-hours basic training, would retain their uniform and would then be required to attend further training sessions as frequently as possible but not less than one session per year. Those unable to fulfil this annual requirement would be discharged. Also introduced were new proficiency tests to follow a revised syllabus of training and the creation of a 'bounty' payment for fully trained members after the completion of 3 years. The 'bounty' was a £10 payment per annum in arrears. There were also new minimum obligations for those who were on the AFS Reserve.

On the 16th January 1968, the Prime Minister announced in a statement to the House of Commons that Civil Defence was to be placed on a 'care and maintenance' basis. Recruitment would cease immediately and the Auxiliary Fire Service, along with other Civil Defence services, would be formally disbanded on the 1st April 1968.

From all over the UK, a stockpile of AFS vehicles, equipment and uniform was taken to various Home Office supply stores. Despite sufficient appliances, equipment and plans in place to meet the predicted effects of a nuclear attack, the recruitment levels of men and women in the AFS never reached national targets. Lack of action and associated boredom was probably one of the biggest factors leading to resignations and lack of interest.

In reality the devastation, fires and fallout resulting from a nuclear attack would have prevented fire crews from getting to within 50 to 100 miles of the scene and safely operate. For conventional bombing attacks there is no doubt that the AFS would have been an effective source of reinforcements, who in particular were very able and proficient at providing water supplies over long distances.

City of Sheffield Auxiliary Fire Service awaiting departure on an exercise to Edinburgh on 25th June 1960
(Source: Mark Johnson Collection)

Industrial Civil Defence Service (ICDS)

The ICDS was a parallel organisation to the CDC; and was founded in 1951 to organise civil defence activities at industrial premises particularly larger factories. Like the CDC; the ICDS utilised and equipped volunteers from individual businesses.

Although no initial financial assistance was available for these industries they did benefit from tax relief on the costs incurred.

CHAPTER 6
EMERGENCY SERVICES

LOCAL FIRE, POLICE & HEALTH CARE PROVISION

Fire Service

The South Yorkshire Fire Service was initially formed out of the four individual District Fire Brigades (Sheffield, Rotherham, Barnsley and Doncaster), which were set up as a result of the Fire Services Act 1947, and which transferred fire-fighting functions from the war-time National Fire Service to fire brigades maintained by the councils of counties and county boroughs.

As a result of the Local Government Act 1972, the four district brigades were formed into a combined South Yorkshire force, being administered by the South Yorkshire County Council created in 1974. From 1986 and as a result of the abolition of the County Council, the fire service passed to the newly formed South Yorkshire Fire & Civil Defence Authority (renamed South Yorkshire Fire & Rescue Authority in 2004). Throughout these changes however the geographical region was maintained as four distinct operational areas.

During the cold war, the fire brigade was (and still is) commanded by a Chief Fire Officer and assisted by staff of Deputy and Assistant Chief Officers. Each division would have had access to a comprehensive range of equipment ranging from pumping appliances, turntable ladders, hose-layers, hydraulic platforms etc.

War Time Response

Between 1948 and 1968, in a war time emergency, all the local authority (Sheffield, Rotherham, Barnsley and Doncaster) brigades would have formed into a combined National Fire Service, commanded by a Regional Fire Commander. The fire brigade would have been assisted by the voluntary Auxiliary Fire Service (see AFS Section) to provide the essential fire fighting functions. As a result of the disbandment of the Civil Defence Corps and

Auxiliary Fire Service in 1968 the fire brigades and later fire service (from the formation of the South Yorkshire County Council), would have undertaken a further range of rescue duties.

Fire Service Mobile Columns

In the precautionary period prior to a potential attack, a number of Mobile Fire columns would be formed and then dispersed to "safe" areas within the County. These would have generally been unused airfields or locations where an adequate level of protection could be provided for staff, vehicles and equipment.

After the disbanding of the Auxiliary Fire Service in 1968, much of the original equipment ranging from "Green Goddess" pumping vehicles, hoses, light portable pumps and inflatable dams were "mothballed" at key Home Office sites ready for immediate distribution during wartime. Concerns existed however, as to the overall effectiveness of the operational potential of mobile columns and ultimately fire provision during the period of conflict. Equipment was limited, staffing was short, and overall effects of the nuclear bomb would have created a situation which would have provided considerable difficulties for undertaking fire fighting duties.

The risk of fallout limited fire-fighting duties, and therefore reliance on effective monitoring of fallout from other key organisations was imperative. Fire fighting duties could only be undertaken as long as there was no risk of fallout. If this was the case then the fires were left to burn themselves out, rather than risking the lives of the fire-fighters.

Also after the Auxiliary Fire Service disbandment, the role of the fire-fighting provision was reappraised and by 1974 a new simpler structure was gradually introduced. This consisted of the peacetime command structure being retained during the period of conflict, however overall control would be in the hands of the Sub Regional Fire Commander located at the SRHQ at Shipton.

The emphasis was placed more on the supply of water through the pumping from water sources such as streams, reservoirs, etc and its subsequent decontamination in order to supply emergency feeding centres, a similar role which would have been undertaken by the Auxiliary Fire Service and which continued through the rest of the cold war period.

Police

During the 1960s a copy of the Police War Duties Handbook was issued to all police staff and would have identified the role required by them if a war emergency arose. In a period of crisis or conventional war, the police would be expected to continue their normal operations although their resources would come under much greater pressure. In addition, early plans envisaged a much wider role even before a nuclear attack.

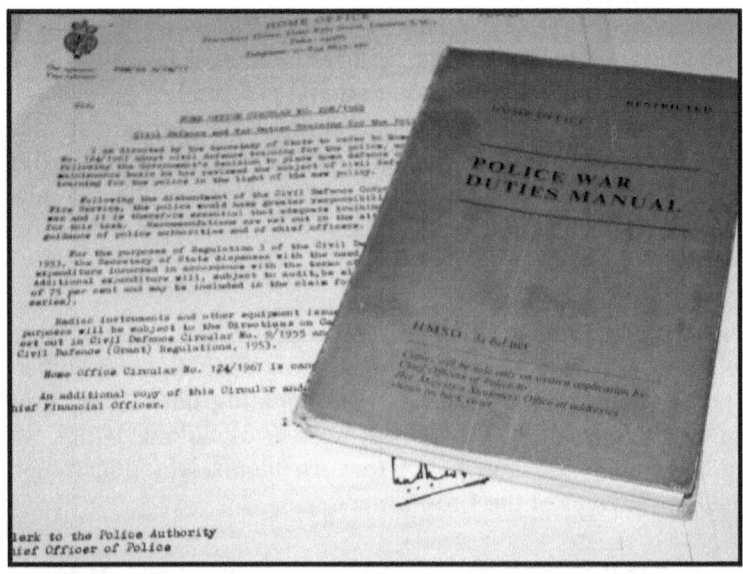

Police War Duties Book & Home Office Circular which would have been issued to Police personnel to guide war duty training.

Command

The Home Secretary designated certain chief constables (see table below) to be Regional Police Commanders. In peace-time they would co-ordinate the police war planning for the region. In war, they would have assumed command of all the police forces within their designated region and be located at the designated Government Headquarters for the region (RWR / RSG / RGHQ). A similarly appointed Sub-Regional Police Commander would have acted as adviser on police matters for the designated sub-region and would have been provided with a small staff operating from the Sub-Regional Control (SRC / SRHQ).

Below Sub Regional level, each police force would have remained under the command of its own Chief Constable.

REGION		FORCE & WAR HQ
1	Northern	Northumbria Police, Newcastle upon Tyne
2	North Eastern	West Yorkshire Police, Wakefield
3	North Midland	Nottinghamshire Constabulary, Nottingham
4	Eastern	Suffolk Constabulary, Ipswich
5	South Eastern	Metropolitan Police, New Scotland Yard
6	Southern	Hampshire Constabulary, Winchester
7	South Western	Avon & Somerset Constabulary, Bristol
8	Wales	South Wales Constabulary, Bridgend
9	Midland	West Midlands Police, Birmingham
10	North Western	Lancashire Constabulary, Preston
	Scotland	Lothian & Borders Police, Edinburgh
	Northern Ireland	Royal Ulster Constabulary, Belfast

Source: Campbell, D; WarPlan UK

Police Responsibilities in an Emergency

When an emergency was declared all police forces would have been mobilised for war duties. Chief Constables would have taken action according to pre-arranged plans and according to specific instructions received from the Home Office. During an emergency, the principal peace-time responsibilities of the police i.e. the prevention of crime, the maintenance of public order, traffic control and general assistance to the public would have continued, but this would have been on an increased scale and involve additional tasks including:-

- Taking special measures to maintain internal security with particular reference to the detention or restriction of potentially subversive people.
- The guarding of key points, protected and prohibited areas and restricting generally the movement of the public.
- Assisting the Armed Forces in their mobilisation plans.
- Staffing carrier control and receiver warning points.
- Supplementing public warnings.
- Assisting in the dispersal of the people in the priority classes i.e. women and children, if the dispersal scheme is made operational.
- Reconnaissance and the control of road traffic.
- Encouraging the public to remain in their homes.

It would have also been the duty of the police to assist in the enforcement of many of the additional restrictions and regulations which it may have been necessary for the Government to impose.

Voluntary Dispersal of People

It has been identified in Chapter 3 that the Government had outlined a scheme for the voluntary dispersal of people to designated dispersal and reception areas. The police would have had the responsibility for the controlling of traffic and crowds within these designated areas and Local Authorities within these areas would have communicated directly with the police to keep them informed with all stages of planning, so as to enable arrangements for traffic and crowd control.

It was the view of the Government that in an emergency the dispersal scheme may not necessarily have been put into action; however in the event, that it was, it may have been necessary depending upon the situation at the time, for police forces in the dispersal area to reinforce those in the reception areas. In the event of an attack while dispersal was in progress, members of the priority classes who had not reached their ultimate destination and were unable to travel further to reach that destination would have to be regarded by the police as homeless and required to billet such groups as quickly as possible as soon as possible (providing situations such as fallout permitted). In all cases the police were to co-operate with the military authorities as far as possible.

Control of Essential Service Routes

From the earliest possible moment after attack the police were entrusted to prevent non-essential road traffic from impacting upon life saving operations. The police would have had a major role in keeping the Essential Service Routes[26] clear and thereby being responsible to control and facilitate the flow of essential services' vehicles and equipment into damaged areas, and to control the movement of homeless and others out of these areas, whether in vehicles or on foot.

Police Mobile Columns

The Police Force had a similar approach to organisation as the Fire Service. Initial plans from 1959 and from the Police War Duties Book of 1965 describe the need for the formation of self-

---

[26] Essential Service Routes (ESR) were originally designated in the 1950s to enable the use of major highway routes for life-saving forces to reach areas of need. By 1967 the plan had been overtaken by events and there would be insufficient forces deemed available. The ESRs were redrawn in 1973, 1976 and 1979 with fewer routes mainly to be kept clear for military mobilisation in the Precautionary Period.

The ESR network neatly embraces the task of providing military logistics routes between major ports, airports, depots and bases, with the task of curbing unwanted civilian flight

supporting mobile police columns with approximately 135 officers who would be dispersed to areas of relative protection.

During the entire cold war period, the need to maximise police strength was deemed essential. If there was an attack on the country then the demands on the police in respect of maintenance of essential service routes, law and order and management of any potential survivors would have been considerable and needed to be supported by adequate resources. This concern eventually led to the decision being made in the mid 1960s to utilise Traffic Wardens to assist the police with their duties. Equipment was always short and in 1967 there was only enough to equip 34 columns. The concept was therefore abandoned and replaced in 1972 with the idea of forming 20% of each force's strength into smaller, more mobile Police Support Units consisting of 35 Officers.

In the 1980s, the police's role in the transition to war phase was emphasised with additional roles in managing traffic, manning the warning system and assisting with the effects of conventional attack. Manpower was to be maximised through the use of Special Constables and Traffic Wardens.

Detention

One such instruction from the mid-1960s covered the detention of suspected persons. The legal authority for this would come from the emergency powers regulations and a master list of political detainees known as the Everest List was kept centrally for the purpose. This generally involved the rounding up of those people who were known or deemed to be potential subversives such as members of hostile "left-wing" political parties including the Communist Party of Great Britain, trade unions.

Health

The role of the National Health Service was extended to cover the treatment of casualties resulting from emergencies, including hostilities. It was however recognised that the sheer scale of casualties and the risk of the potential loss of many of the medical sites i.e. hospitals, surgeries etc could be very considerable, leaving a potential problem for the maintenance of care for the surviving casualties.

Wherever possible such services would aim to be maintained as far as possible through the use of doctors, dental practitioners, key medical groups such as the St. Johns Ambulance and British Red Cross or other medically equipped organisation.

These resources would be brought together and organised into specific Emergency Medical Centres which would be sited strategically within the community, and key communication links between hospitals and medical centres would be maintained using the Ambulance service resources. In the event of a large number of casualties the use of triage would be used at these sites i.e. to prioritise patients based on the severity of their condition. This effectively rations patient treatment efficiently when resources are insufficient for all to be treated immediately as would most probably be the case after a nuclear attack.

Casualties would therefore be classified into one of three groups[27];

1. Survivors in need of no further medical attention.
2. Those survivors requiring "limited surgical procedures" and deemed to have a good probability of surviving the first seven days and to have a fair chance of recovery.
3. Those requiring major surgery or medical attention and deemed to be unable to survive in the short term.

In the worst possible situation, the availability of key medical centres may be non-existent, and therefore community facilities would need to be developed in which the casualties would be cared for by the community. In many cases no medical facilities would be available. It would be the sole responsibility of the community to organise its own facilities including a First Aid Centre and Community Nursing Centre.

---

[27] Information from Campbell, D. War Plan UK p310

CHAPTER 7
UTILITIES

MAINTAINING POWER, WATER & COMMUNICATIONS

Energy Provision

Basic Primary Fuels

The pattern of energy demand in a period of tension and in conventional war would be different than from peacetime. Significant proportions of the demand would be considered unnecessary and non-essential use could be restricted by government direction using existing peacetime powers. Restrictions could also be imposed on essential users, particularly in relation to gas. Energy supplies and stocks are unlikely to be direct targets for conventional attack except where they are of importance to military operations. The complexity and inter-dependence of the manufacture and distribution of energy makes the industry very vulnerable to serious disruption following a general nuclear attack.

Within the cold war, (and just as relevant today), the main forms of energy focus around primary energy sources including:-

- Coal
- Crude oil
- Natural gas
- Nuclear

These energy sources when converted, burnt or transformed through power stations create the electricity that we all use for powering electronic devices.

Electricity Generation

In the UK there are approximately 250 generating stations burning coal and oil, approximately 80 hydro-electric stations and an handful of nuclear stations all producing in the range of between 50 to 2000 MW of power. During the cold war the generation of electricity was the role of the Central Electricity Generating Board (from 1957 to privatisation in 1990) who also had the task of controlling and maintaining the trunk transmission grid network of 132, 275 and 400 Kilovolt lines in England and Wales (approximately 19,000 circuit miles) through approximately 800 switching stations. In Scotland electricity generation was carried out by the South of Scotland Electricity Board and the North of Scotland Hydro-Electric Board.

The network was split up into Area Boards[28] in England and Wales who were responsible for the overhead and underground distribution networks totalling approximately 315,000 circuit miles and for the retail sale of electricity to the consumers within their area i.e. businesses and residents. The Area Board covering South Yorkshire would have been located at Leeds. At the centre of the CEGB's infrastructure was the National Control Room of the National Grid located in London, which was part of the control hierarchy for the system at that time. At the time, more than one-third of the electricity generated was for industrial purposes, slightly less for residential use with the remainder being used for public services. After a potential nuclear attack the energy system would have been most vulnerable and no matter what level this attack would have taken, the damage to the supply system would have been considerable.

The effect of a nuclear device exploding causes a massive generation of electric and magnetic fields which coupled with electrical / electronic systems produces damaging current and voltage surges. This is usually referred to as an Electro-Magnetic Pulse (EMP) (see earlier chapter). The strongest part of the pulse lasts for only a fraction of a second, but any unprotected electrical

---

[28] Originally centred at Newcastle upon Tyne, Leeds, Manchester, Nottingham, Birmingham, St Albans, East Grinstead and Bristol

equipment — and anything connected to electrical cables, which act as giant lightning rods or antennas — will be affected by the pulse. Older systems which relied upon vacuum tube (valve) based equipment was seen to be much less vulnerable to EMP. The impact of this EMP which would cause severe damage to the generation and distribution network to business and residents coupled with the subsequent effects of nuclear fallout would lead to a significant time for such equipment and network to be repaired.

Water

Water forms the primary requirement for survival; without a clean water supply, the chances of survival would be limited. It is therefore essential that clean water provision is maintained. The country is divided by nature into rainfall catchment areas, and it is these areas which have generally developed into the areas of ten regional water authorities. These water authorities were formed by the introduction of the Water Act in 1973, which merged the previous smaller district water boards within the area. The key role of each water authority was the provision of water supply within the area; however they also provide and maintain the sewerage system including the treatment and disposal of waste and provide land drainage and recreational use of water sources such as reservoirs.

Within South Yorkshire, as a result of the Water Act 1973 the former water boards belonging to Sheffield, Barnsley, Rotherham and Doncaster District Authorities were formed into the Yorkshire Water Authority whose boundary stretches from Richmond, Northallerton and Whitby in the North to Sheffield and Rotherham in the South and separated to the West by the backbone of the UK mainland; the Pennines.

Supplies

Depending on the area, water is generally sourced from underground sources, which form as a result of the infiltration of water through rocks high in the hills. This water having passed through a range of filtering sands and rocks requires minimal treatment. The rest of the water is sourced directly from rivers and is treated within water treatment works, before being stored in reservoirs.

The "Alert" Period

During the "Alert" period, an attack is deemed imminent. All resources should be conserved wherever possible to ensure that adequate supplies are available, and that the systems used to deliver such supplies are protected.

During this period the water authority would undertake the following actions;

- The suspension of the removal of water from rivers / water sources.
- The reduction in stored water (within storage reservoirs) to minimise the risk of flooding caused as a result of a breach in reservoirs.
- The number of pumps in use restricted to conserve power.
- All interconnections between reservoirs and works shut.
- All mains and trunk mains should be progressively reduced to maintain supply.

The "Post-Attack" Period

The general situation as a result of an attack on an area will be unlike anything ever experienced before, and the overall difficulties faced by water organisations would be almost impossible to comprehend. Where the effects of fallout did not inhibit such organisations from operating; such organisations would need to undertake a number of key localised obligations ranging from fire fighting, flood control and rescue; however the ultimate key responsibility would be for the provision of safe water for the population.

The Water Authority would use whatever resources were available and assisted by the emergency services such as fire (for water pumping) to ensure a minimum water supply of 2 pints of drinking water and at least 2 gallons of water for drinking, cooking and hygiene requirements per person per day. Although water authorities developed plans in respect to a potential nuclear attack, it was not until the mid 1980s when protected facilities started to be developed. During the mid 1980s the Yorkshire Water Authority commissioned the construction of ten[29] protected bunkers which were developed to ensure that water infrastructure, equipment and personnel would be available after the attack. These bunkers were based on a Swiss design and incorporated protection and facilities to allow engineers to maintain and manage water facilities after an attack.

Telecommunications

History and Formation

The creation of the GPO's (General Post Office) "Postal Telegraphs Department" as a result of the passing of the Telegraph Act 1868 formed the initial main body that was to manage and control the telephone network to the present day. The GPO which combined a number of small telegraph companies initially controlled the main telegraph system for the UK. It was not until the invention of the telephone in 1876 that the GPO began to provide telephone services from some of its telegraph exchanges.

Over the next two decades the telephone system grew initially under the GPO in some areas and through private ownership in others. The National Telephone Company emerged as a result of the absorption of these smaller private companies and formed the main competitor to the GPO before being acquired and combined with the GPO in 1912.

Two initial telephone networks existed within the UK:-

- **Trunk Network:** formed the main system covering the UK. This network was unified under GPO control in 1896.
- **Local Network:** formed the main networks which linked to the trunk network but covered smaller geographic areas.

---

[29] It is believed that Yorkshire Water constructed two sites within South Yorkshire at Sheffield and Doncaster. Out of these sites information is only available on the Sheffield site based at the Langsett Water Treatment Works to the North of Sheffield.

This network was unified under GPO control in 1912, however a few municipally-owned services remained outside of GPO control e.g. Kingston-upon-Hull.

In 1969 the GPO; a government department, became the Post Office, a nationalised industry separate from government and Post Office Telecommunications formed one of its divisions. In 1977, a report was produced into the review of Post Office services. The report was headed by Sir Charles Frederick Carter and his committee ("Carter Committee") recommended a separation of the two main services of the GPO and for their relocation under two individual corporations rather than being as divisions within the GPO.

The findings contained in the report led to the "British Telecom" brand being introduced in 1980 and on 1 October 1981, this became the official name of Post Office Telecommunications and becoming a state-owned corporation, independent of the Post Office. At this time the first steps were taken to introduce competition into the UK telecommunications industry and in 1982 BT's monopoly on telecommunications was broken, with the granting of a licence to Mercury Communications. Later the British Telecommunications Act, 1981 transferred the responsibility for telecommunications services from the Post Office, creating two separate corporations.

Operations

The telephone network is a complex set of wires linked between a main Trunk and Local communication networks. The local networks originally formed the first links for subscribers who were linked through to main telephone exchanges through the overhead telephone wires. These main exchanges then connected the user through to the main trunk network. Prior to 1958 this process of linking the networks was undertaken by a number of operators located at the telephone exchanges; however from 1958 the process (known as Subscriber Trunk Dialling [STD]) was automated to allow a through link between the networks for the user without the need to link to an operator. In 1976 the last manual exchange in the United Kingdom at Portree in the Isle of Skye closed making the British telephone system fully automatic.

In an emergency

The main function of the GPO / BT during an emergency would be to ensure the maintenance of the telephone services. The majority of the telephone network relies greatly on the telephone wires that link down streets to the subscribers' residences and businesses. During a nuclear attack many of the wires maintaining the telephone network would have been vulnerable to the blast on a nuclear device and the electronics used for the system, affected by the EMP that the nuclear device generates. It was therefore essential that a system was in place to maintain telecommunications facilities for central / regional government.

During the 1950s two schemes were planned and implemented with the main objective to increase both the capacity and survivability of the line circuits used for telephone and telegraph. The first involved moving the telephone system away from any potential risk from the blast effects of the nuclear bomb or its subsequent damaging EMP. To achieve this, six underground exchanges were planned. These included:-

- London
- Birmingham
- Manchester
- Liverpool
- Glasgow
- Leeds

In reality only three were constructed;

- London (Kingsway) c.1954
- Manchester (Guardian) c. 1955
- Birmingham (Anchor) c. 1957

These exchanges consisted of a number of tunnels linked to the main exchange and like the many nuclear "bunkers" around the country at the time were constructed of concrete which was capable to withstand the effects of a nuclear blast and which were reinforced with high tensile steel reinforcement bars which were linked to provide a protective cage (known as a "Faraday cage"). A second system which was initially planned in 1954 (operational in the early 1960s) consisted of a series of cable and microwave transmitters which were designed to maintain long distance communication in the event of an attack.

"Backbone" Microwave Transmitter at Windy Hill on the border between Lancashire and Yorkshire and accessible from Junction 22 of the M62 Motorway
(Source: S W Craine, 2009)

Microwave Transmitter at Tinshill, Leeds. Although not on the "Backbone" link, it did provide key microwave communication links parallel to the network.
(Source: Noel, J Ryan)

These transmitters formed the "Backbone" system and were generally located in areas deemed to offer a less risk of damage from targeted nuclear weapons and formed a skeleton of links running from the South of the UK up the country to the North of Scotland. Although such sites varied depending upon the locations they generally constructed in concrete for those sites deemed at greater risk of damage (usually within the inner urban areas) or steel "pylon" style which were deemed of less risk of damage in the event of an attack (usually in more rural areas). Further microwave links offered duplicate / parallel links from the Backbone network.

"Preferential Treatment"

Prior to or during any major emergency, the sheer volume of usage of the telecommunication system would generally overburden the system, to a degree in which it would be impossible to manage the system effectively and potentially hamper the roles of the life saving organisations. As a result, the GPO / BT developed a hierarchy of usage ranging from those organisations and people in greatest need for usage of the network to the least. This system; which was known as the Telephone Preference System was introduced in 1962 and consisted of the prioritising of the users of the public telephone lines into 3 groups:-

- **Group A:** All in this group consisted of all non-essential users. This group consisted of approximately 90% of lines. The restriction of the telephone lines to these groups left the existing lines free for Groups B and C.

- **Group B:** All in this group consisted of those users who were required and necessary for life saving purposes within a community. Public phone boxes are included. These consisted of approximately 8% of lines.

- **Group C:** All in this group consisted of those users who were required for the effective co-ordination and control for maintaining national survival after an attack. These consisted of approximately 2% of lines.

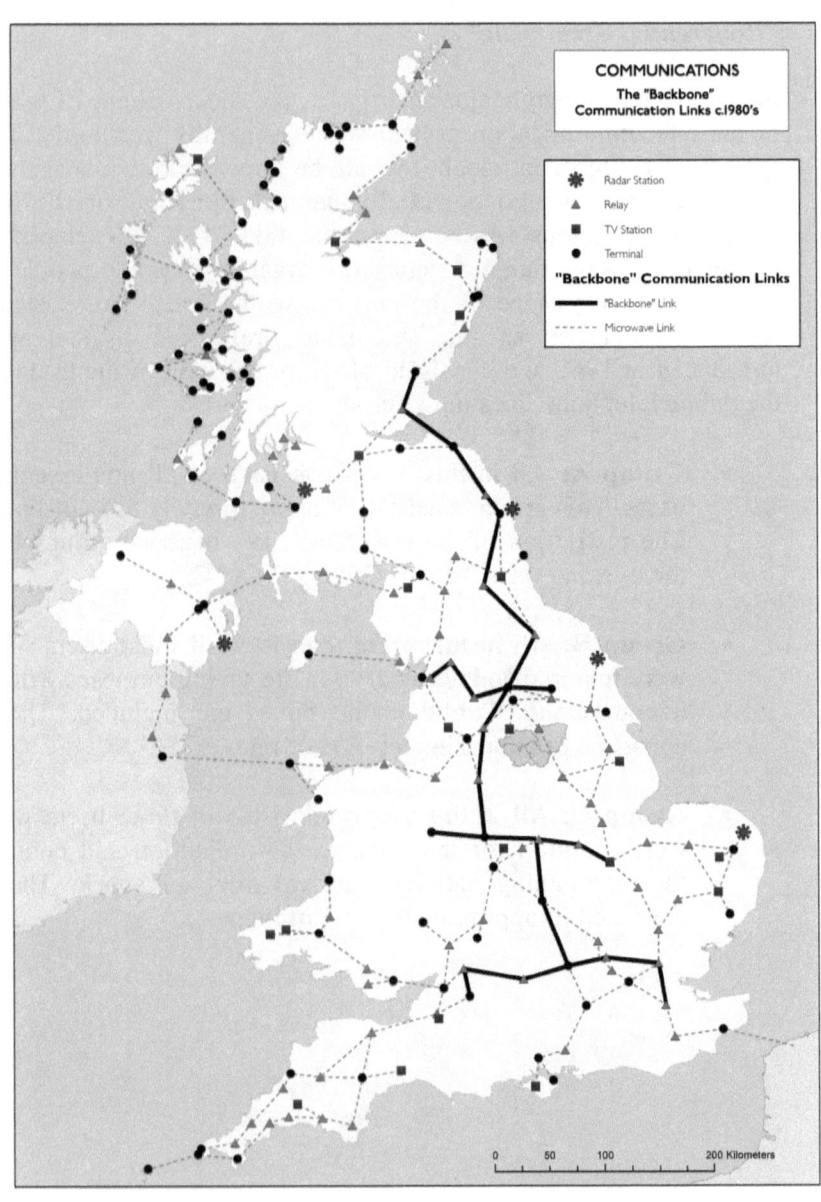

The "Backbone" Communication System c.1980s. The way in which the network bypasses South Yorkshire can clearly be seen.
Source: Based on the "Backbone" system as described in Duncan Campbell's Warplan UK

SECTION 4

INFRASTRUCTURE SURVEY

TO RECAP ...

The previous section highlighted the key organisations which assisted the central / regionalised government with information to allow them to make effective decisions with regards to the management and control of personnel, facilities and resources before, during and after a nuclear attack on the country. It has also been identified that a number of differing layers of government control exist; ranging from central / regional levels through to a more localised area.

In respect to South Yorkshire, these controlling levels were particularly prevalent; some with greater control than others and all requiring some form of key site in which to control the region or manage the resources to aid the population. The following section therefore focuses on the sites that would have had some influence on the management of South Yorkshire during a war situation.

The following sections aim to highlight these sites. In some cases little is known regarding the sites as they are still under strict secrecy. Where this is the case, then the general locations of the sites will be identified and their role identified.

CHAPTER 8

REGIONAL / LOCAL AUTHORITY SITES
(Inc. Civil Defence)

General Locations

During the Cold War the chain of command in place formed a structure which necessitated the effective management of the region and local areas. Throughout this period South Yorkshire would have been managed from a number of sites, which varied depending upon changes within Government Policy, finance, and changing in operating procedures such as the disbandment of the Civil Defence Corps.

Regionalised Government such as Regional War Room / Regional Seat of Government or Sub-Regional Headquarters covering South Yorkshire were generally centralised within areas of West or North Yorkshire. These effectively controlled the "region" at the highest level of control. At a more local level, protected accommodation was located within the district area e.g. Sheffield, Barnsley, Rotherham and Doncaster.

REGIONAL AUTHORITY

Regional War Rooms (1953 – 1965)

Site Description

The initial War Rooms were built to a standard design which was based on those developed by the RAF and Royal Observer Corps Operations Rooms during WW2. The design is based on a two-storey building offering approximately 9500 square feet of space. The majority of the buildings were built on the surface so that all levels were exposed, however all external and internal walls were constructed of reinforced concrete capable to withstand an atomic bomb blast. The external walls were 5ft thick and designed to withstand a direct hit from a 500-pound bomb

A small number such as at Leeds had lower floors which were located beneath ground level which generally would have provided greater protection, but in many cases such suffered from water ingress in later life. The rooms were arranged around a central two-storey map room which was overlooked by a series of control cabins on the first floor. The rooms were equipped with their own generator and air filters; communications equipment and although not intended for continuous occupation they included dormitories equipped with 2-tier metal bunks, showers, a canteen and kitchen.

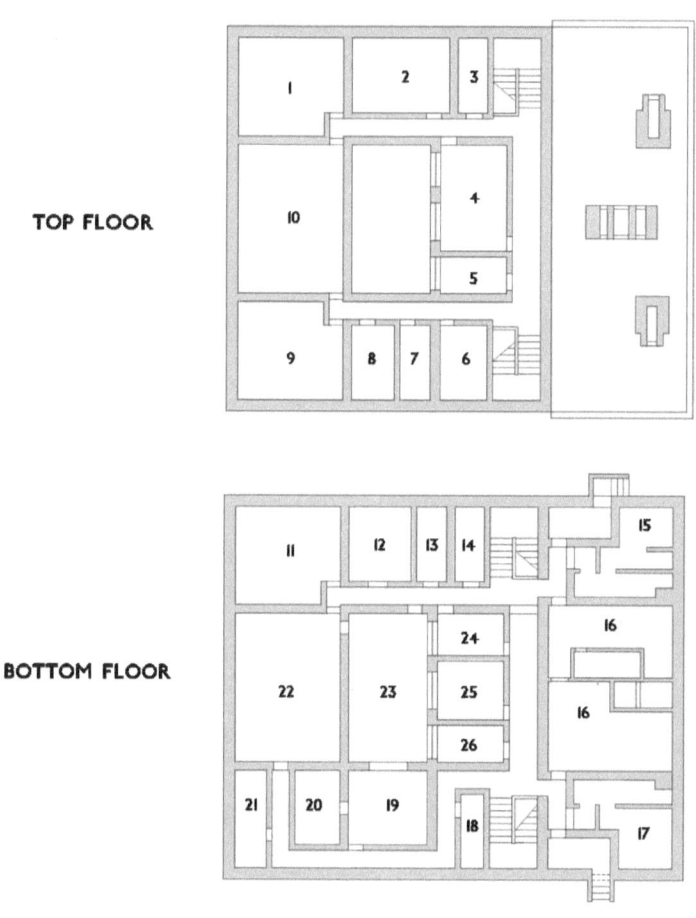

Typical Plan of a Regional War Room
(Manual representation of plans by Cocroft & Thomas, 2004)

1/2	Office	15	Female Toilets
3	Water Storage	16	Plant Room
4/5	Control Cabin	17	Male Toilets
6	Office	18	Entry Control
7	Water Storage	19/20	Control Cabin
8/9/10	Office	21	Dormitory (M)
11	Dormitory (F)	22	Canteen
12/13	Telephone Exchange	23	Map Room
14	Entry Control	24/25/26	Control Cabin

Locations of Sites

Name:	**LEEDS (War Room Area 2)**
Location:	**Lawnswood, Leeds, West Yorkshire**
Type of Building:	**War Room**
OS Grid Reference:	**SE27063887**

The Leeds Regional War Room is located on the government estate at Lawnswood to the North of Leeds City Centre and on the East side of Otley Road opposite Lawnswood Crematorium. The site is a semi-sunk bunker in which the lower level is underground while the upper level is above ground.

The War Room opened in early 1950s but within a few years developments with regards to nuclear bombs had rendered the site almost obsolete with the regional control passing to the Regional Seat of Government site at Imphal Barracks in York by 1958 and the site being transferred to the Regional Seat of Government subordinate control. After 1968 it was no longer required until 1981 when the upper level was refitted as Leeds City Council Control however suffering from water ingress and subsequent damp, the lower level was not used by the Council.

During the late 1980s / 90s the site was considered by security company Cerberus who provide key holding and alarm response with dedicated patrol officers. Cerberus had also originally considered the former 18 Group ROC Group Control building at Yeadon (see later). These sites were not acquired by Cerberus and the site now stands empty.

Aerial Photo of Leeds Regional War Room in 2006
(Source: Mark Johnson Collection)

Regional Seats of Government (1950s -1960s)

Site Description and Location

Name:	YORK - IMPHAL BKS (RSG Area 2)
Location:	North Yorkshire
Type of Building:	Military Army Barracks
OS Grid Reference:	SE60905015

York's Regional Seat of Government was located within the main Imphal Barracks complex at Fulford to the South of York City Centre. It is believed that the site has an extensive underground operations room; however because of the "secretive" nature of the site this cannot be confirmed.

Sub-Regional Control / Sub-Regional Headquarters / Regional Government Headquarters (1970s – 1980s)

Name:	CONISBOROUGH (SRC Area 22)
Location:	North Yorkshire
Type of Building:	AAOR
OS Grid Reference:	SK49109711

Conisborough Sub-Regional Control site is located 10 Kilometres south-west of Doncaster Town Centre and utilises the former Anti-Aircraft Operations Room as developed post WW2. The building having been decommissioned in the 1960s was acquired for redevelopment and is now a private residence.

Aerial Photo of Conisborough AAOR / SRC site in 2005
(Source: Mark Johnson Collection)

The plan below shows the layout of such a site during its original operational phase.

TOP FLOOR
(ABOVE GROUND LEVEL)

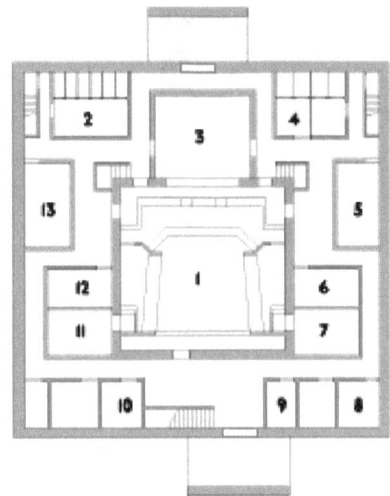

BOTTOM FLOOR
(BELOW GROUND LEVEL)

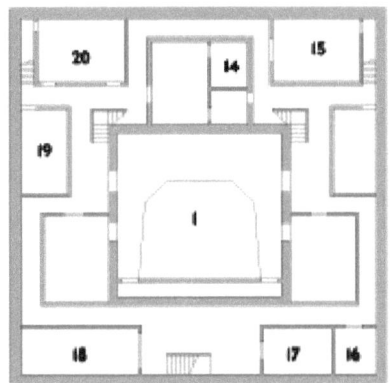

Typical Plan of an AAOR Control
(Manual representation of plans by Cocroft & Thomas, 2004)

1	Main Plotting Area	12	WRAC Officers Office
2	Toilets	13	Rest Room
3	Switchboards	14	Battery Store
4	Toilets	15	Office
5/6	Rest Room	16	Boiler Room
7	NAAFI	17	Air Conditioning Room
8	Clerks Office	18	Generator Room
9	Guard room	19	Electrical Swich Room
10	Signals Office	20	WRAC Rest Room
11	Civil Servants Office		

Name:	SHIPTON (SRHQ Area 21 & RGHQ Area 21)
Location:	Shipton by Beningborough, North Yorkshire
Type of Building:	R4 Rotor Building
OS Grid Reference:	SE54266181
Operational Period:	1962

Shipton was originally developed as a R4 Rotor site in 1953. These Rotor sites were designed to exercise the intermediate control and reporting functions under Fighter Command HQ located at RAF Bentley Priory.

The Rotor system in the UK was structured into six operational sectors, each of which consisted of a Sector Operations Centre, which along with Fighter Command received information from radar stations and ROC Group HQs of any potential attack.

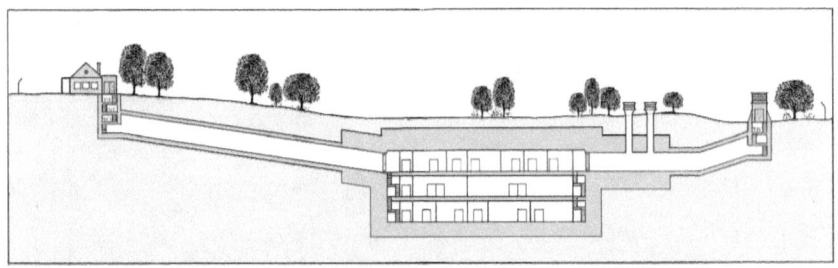

Example of layout of a 3-Level Rotor Bunker
(Redrawn, updated and based on the original within WarPlan UK by Duncan Campbell)

The site was vacated by the RAF in the early 1960s and converted in 1962 as a Sub-Regional Headquarters (SRHQ 21) covering the North East of England area. Between 1976 and 1981 the site underwent a further refit, when a fourth floor was added above the top floor mainly to provide extra dormitory space. To construct this new upper level it was necessary to cut through the 10 foot thick reinforced concrete roof of the original bunker. The new upper level was then covered by a substantial earth mound. Shipton was later redesigned as RGHQ 2.1 one of two RGHQs in Region 2 (The other was at Hexham).

Shipton SRHQ guardhouse building in 2009.
(Source: Noel J Ryan)

Shipton SRHQ site in 2009 from the main A19 trunk road
(Source: Noel J Ryan)

Shipton SRHQ from above showing the top of the bunker after removal of the protected earth

(Source: Mark Johnson Collection)

LOCAL AUTHORITY

Name:	SOUTH YORKSHIRE COUNTY COUNCIL
Location:	Cusworth Hall, Doncaster County Hall, Barnsley
OS Grid References:	SE54900395 SE34640637
Operational Period:	1970s – 1980s

During the 1970s / 80s the South Yorkshire County Council was based at Kendray Street, Barnsley at the County Hall. South Yorkshire's six-storey County Hall at Kendray Street, Barnsley, is now renamed Central Offices and is used by Barnsley Borough Council's housing, planning, and public services departments.

The 1960s building had originally been leased from Norwich Union and then sub-let to the County Council to ensure that Barnsley remained the county town. As part of its Civil Protection requirements, during a nuclear war, the council would have developed a main War HQ located to the West of Doncaster at the stately house; Cusworth Hall. During this time the County Hall in Barnsley would have been used as a standby wartime HQ to assist the main HQ.

Cusworth Hall near Doncaster. It is believed that this site would have occupied the War Room for South Yorkshire County Council. The site is now a living history museum.
(Source: Noel J Ryan)

Former South Yorkshire County Council – County Hall and now owned by Barnsley Metropolitan Borough Council and due for imminent demolition
(Source: Noel J Ryan)

Name:	**ROTHERHAM** (Local Authority)
Location:	South Yorkshire
Type of Building:	Former CD Building
OS Grid Reference:	SK45249413
Operational Period:	1950s – 1960s

Rotherham, at least initially, provided more robust premises in the form of a specially constructed bunker. The "Rotherham Borough Control" as it was known was located in a compound behind the junction of the A630 and A6123 roads.

The bunker was built around 1954 and should have been available for use until the end of the cold war, in a similar fashion to Doncaster's (see below). It was however not used since the disbanding of the Civil Defence Corps in 1968. The bunker was supposed to have been kept on 'care and maintenance' but with increasing reluctance towards civil defence expenditure, it was left to slowly fall into an irreparable state.

Sadly the bunker was totally demolished in October 2007 to make way for new flats development.

The Rotherham bunker, 2007 (above and below)
(Source: Noel J Ryan)

View down one of the internal corridors
(Source: Noel J Ryan)

Various internal views of the bunker photographed prior to demolition
(above and below)
(Source: Noel J Ryan))

Name:	SHEFFIELD (Local Authority)
Location:	Sheffield, South Yorkshire
Type of Building:	NON-EXISTANT
OS Grid Reference:	SK35438703
Operational Period:	Unknown

Sheffield: "Nuclear Free"

During the 1970s and 1980s Sheffield has had a long opposition to nuclear weapons and during the 1980s visitors to the City could not miss the signs on the sides of the roads identifying Sheffield (like a number of other towns and cities across the region) as a "NUCLEAR FREE ZONE".

During the 1970s and 1980s a number of grants relating to Nuclear Free Zone activities were made by the City Council. These are identified as being for[30];

- £10,000 for producing an up-dated version of the BBC film "The War Game"
- £750 for producing and presenting an anti-nuclear scenario for Sheffield.
- £100 for affiliation fees to the "Anti Trident Campaign".
- £915 for a research project on Civil Defence.
- £500 for office equipment and £20,000 for rental subsidy for the Sheffield Peace Shop.
- £200 for a production of "When the Wind Blows" by the Skylight theatre company.
- £200 for printing postcards saying "Sheffield (a Nuclear Free Zone)
- £4000 for mailing every household in Sheffield with the leaflet " You & the Bomb"
- £1000 to SANA for "Nuclear Winter Initiatives
- £1000 to Sheffield peace liaison committee
- £1000 to the NFZ steering committee.
- £510 to "Various individuals" to make anti-nuclear films & videos.

---

[30] Information from the website of the Hack Green Secret Nuclear Bunker.

- £2673 to "Various individuals" in connection with NFZ &CND conferences.
- £850 for the production & £1115 for the purchase of anti-nuclear videotapes.
- £793 for the "Sheffield Peace Film Group"
- £200 for the purchase of cassettes of "One World Peace Song)
- £90000 1982-85. Salary for Mr Jim Coleman. Sheffield Peace Officer.

In October 1980, the Sheffield Star Newspaper published a series of Articles entitled: "The Bomb and You." In these Articles Sheffield Star journalist Martin Dawes wrote;

"Sheffield is a major city. In a recent Home Defence 'war games' it was assumed a three megaton bomb made a direct hit on the city and killed 130,000 people outright. Another 80,000 were trapped or injured ..."

"... Thousands more died from radiation in the days and weeks that followed. Directly after an attack there would be no-one to help us. The Government has made it clear it is staying undercover until it is safe to come out".

So did Sheffield have a nuclear bunker for the City Council?

Many believe because of its objection to Nuclear Weapons that it didn't, however there have been many comments suggesting that it did and the most likely location was in the basement of the former Town Hall extension commonly known to "Sheffielders" as the "Eggbox". The "Eggbox" was engineered by Sheffield Engineering Consultants "Husband & Co."[31] and completed in 1977.

The building was built to a radical design which did not gain favour with some Sheffield residents. It was nevertheless different and complete with a roof-top garden, cost approximately £9 million

---

[31] Husband & Co who engineered the "Bridge on the River Kwai" for the film is now part of consultancy company Mott MacDonald.

to construct. It however lasted only 27 years being demolished in 2002.

Initial plans of the "Eggbox" did incorporate an underground car-park in its basement, which was accessed by a ramp at the side of the building at street level and IF there were a bunker then this would be the likely area. In the event of an attack, the underground car park would have provided at least some protection from a nuclear blast and could have been hastily prepared for action. It is however questionable as to whether a purpose built structure did exist especially one which incorporated general "bunker" features such as blast proof doors, filtered air system and living space[32].

Name:	BARNSLEY (Local Authority)
Location:	South Yorkshire
Type of Building:	Unknown
OS Grid Reference:	Unknown
Operational Period:	Unknown

No information has been found as to the location of a protected site within Barnsley for Barnsley Local Authority, however as the South Yorkshire County Council and its standby HQ was located close to the Town Hall site on Kendray Street, it is assumed that any emergency control would be linked to that of the County Council.

Please refer to the South Yorkshire County Council Entry above

---

[32] The authors would be interested to hear from anyone who knows more about this.

Name:	DONCASTER (Local Authority)
Location:	South Yorkshire
Type of Building:	Purpose Built
OS Grid Reference:	SE57360294
Operational Period:	1960s -1970s

The Doncaster Borough Control is located in the basement of the present Coroner's Court building on Union Street in the Centre of Doncaster. The building which now houses the Coroners Court was constructed in the early 1960s and is still in good internal condition having being refurbished for its current use.

The protected accommodation still exists in the buildings' basement albeit now used, in part, for the storage of Coroner's files. The back door of the building fronts on to Cleveland Street and it's possible to see the first gas tight door from the street. This is at the top of the stairs leading down into the basement.

Doncaster Coroners Court Building; formerly Doncaster MBC Borough Emergency Control (Above and Below)
(Source: Noel J Ryan))

CHAPTER 9

ROYAL OBSERVER CORPS STRUCTURES

GROUP CONTROLS

Site Description and Plans

Prior to 1961, many of the ROC Group Controls were surface level building and being generally developed during WW2 offered little protection to a nuclear bomb. From 1960 new purpose built semi-sunk Group Control buildings were planned and constructed. These buildings consisted of a three-level reinforced concrete building which has been covered by an earth mound up to the height of the middle floor. The structure of the building is as follows;

- **Top Level:** Entrance to the building is via a flight of steps which leads up to the top floor and unprotected level of the building. This top level, being above the protection of the earth banking is constructed with thicker walls to withstand the greater impact of a nuclear blast. The top level contains the initial airlock and decontamination room to restrict any access of nuclear fallout into the building. Also in the top level is the water tank which would provide enough water for at least two weeks supply, during an emergency situation.

- **Middle Level:** The middle floor contains the main residential area of the building, including; toilets, male and female dormitories, officers room as well as plant room, ejector room for sewerage, telephone frame room, kitchen and rest rooms. Also on this floor is the top level of the plotting room, which provides access onto the balcony where all the burst and fallout information from the posts was collated. Burst times, pressure reading, bearings and elevations were plotted on the triangulation table and fallout readings were plotted on tote boards. In groups equipped with "AWDREY", the computer was located near to the triangulation table on this level.

- **Bottom Level:** The bottom floor contains the main communications for the control including switchboard, warning keyboard, 'Display for Europe' and the fallout decay plotting boards. The bottom floor also incorporates the plotting area which provides access to the Displays A and B for assessing the impact and path of nuclear fallout across the country and contains the working area for the UKWMO Warning Officers who provided the scientific advice.

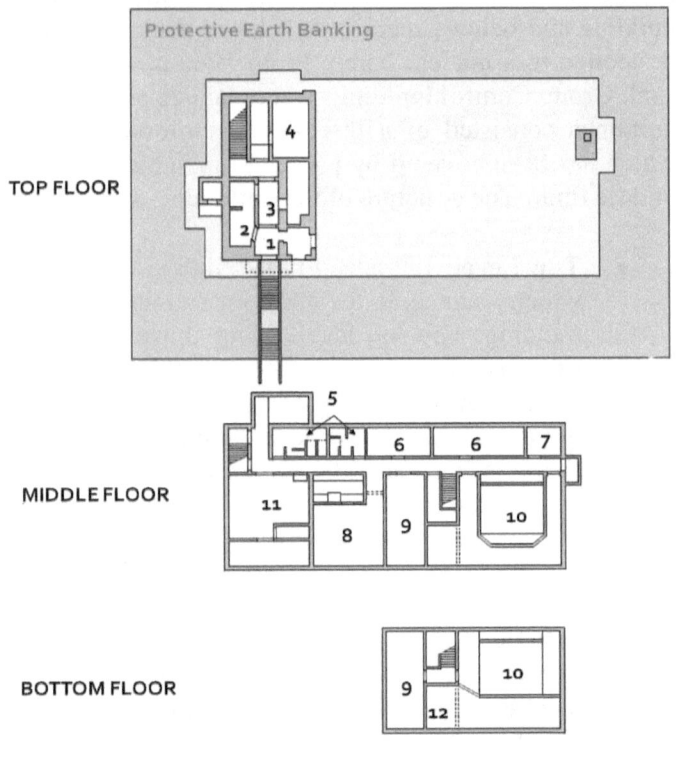

1	Entrance	7	Officers Room
2	Decontamination Room	8	Canteen / Kitchen Area
3	Airlock	9	Communications
4	Water Storage	10	Plotting Area
5	Toilets	11	Plant Room
6	Dormitories	12	Alcove

Plan of ROC Group Control showing main key operational rooms
(Manual representation of plans by Cocroft & Thomas, 2004)

Site Locations

Overground Group Control

Name:	YORK[33] (9 / 10 Group)
Location:	Knavesmire, York
OS Grid Reference:	SE59305070
Operational Period:	1943 – 1961

The original York ROC Group Control HQ can be found on common land at Knavesmire on the south side of York. Constructed by renowned York builders; William Birch & Sons, the building was completed and opened in 1943. The building was one of two similar buildings, built 100 yards apart, each controlling an original ROC Group (9 & 10).

The 10 Group HQ was operational until a reorganisation in November 1953 saw parts of 10 Group merge with 9 Group to become 20 Group. The 10 Group HQ was then closed and has now been demolished. The building offered a small level of protection, however when compared to the destructive power of an Atomic bomb, was deemed to be minimal and although the original 9 Group HQ would see service as the 20 Group HQ it was finally replaced in 1961 by a new semi-sunken and protected control bunker at Acomb, York (see below).

The first purpose built ROC Group Control at Knavesmire, York. Now used as a changing room for a Rugby Club. (Source: Noel J Ryan)

---

[33] Although this site was not directly related to South Yorkshire, by 1968 a number of South Yorkshire sites were under the control of the new protected site in York. It has been included to provide context.

Name:	**LEEDS (8 Group)**
Location:	**Leeds**
OS Grid Reference:	**SE28953573**
Operational Period:	**1940s – 1960s**

The first 8 Group ROC control was based at the GPO building on Vicar Lane, Leeds in 1939 before being transferred to Grove House, Grosvenor Road, Hyde Park in Leeds in 1942.

Grove House was located within the Leeds District of Hyde Park and consisted of a similar structure as the York (10 Group Control building at Knavesmire, York (see above).

The building was used through the continuation of the war until the need for protected accommodation (as a result of the development of nuclear warfare), led to a new purpose built site being developed on the outskirts of North Leeds close to the former Avro plant and airport at Yeadon.

Shortly after transfer of the Group Control to Yeadon; it is believed that the building was demolished as a result of significant costs for extensive repairs to the building; however it is unclear as to whether any part of the building survived.

Although much of the building no longer exists, the original boundary wall to the site is still in situ and a number of former garden buildings are in use by the University of Leeds as their Grove House Experimental Garden with a number of glass houses on the site. Further areas of the site now house blocks of flats.

Now used as residential apartments for students on the site of the former Grove House. (Source: Noel J Ryan)

Underground Group Controls

Name:	COVENTRY (8 Group)
Location:	Lawford Heath, Rugby
OS Grid Reference:	SP45707360
Operational Period:	1963 – 1992

8 Group ROC HQ is located on the edge of the former RAF Lawford Heath a few miles outside Rugby. After ROC stand-down in 1991, the bunker and the substantial administration block became Regional Government HQ 9.2 (refer to RGHQ section). This was however short lived and by 1993 the building had become redundant and was sold to a local business partnership for £50,000. Over the next few years it quickly fell into disrepair after being used for illegal raves and parties.

In 1997 the site was sold to Teleport UK Ltd t/a Satellite Media Services who provided international internet and satellite services. The administration block was completely refurbished and altered so that it was barely recognisable from its original form. In 2005 the site (known as "Earth Station") was offered for sale by property consultants GVA Grimley on behalf of the administrators of Teleport UK Ltd. As a result, in 2006 the Teleport operations and site was acquired by Satellite Mediaport Services (SMS) satellite and communications company and was further extensively refurbished.

ROC 8 Group Control at Lawford Heath at Stand-down September 1991
(Source: SY ROC Museum)

Coventry ROC 8 Group Control at Lawford Heath on 21st July 1995
(Source: John Gedge via ROC Museum)

*Coventry ROC 8 Group Control Open Day on the 6th Oct 1988
Shows DGC Obs/Lt/Cdr Martin Burgess on steps*
(Source: Jon Layne via ROC Museum)

The former ROC 8 Group Control at Lawford Heath in 2009
(Source: Satellite MediaPort Services)

The former ROC 8 Group Control at Lawford Heath in 2006
(Source: Satellite MediaPort Services)

The former ROC 8 Group Control at Lawford Heath in 2006
(Source: Satellite MediaPort Services)

The former ROC 8 Group Control at Lawford Heath in 2006
(Source: Satellite MediaPort Services)

The former lower floor of the plotting area of 8 Group Control at Lawford Heath in 2008.
(Source: Satellite MediaPort Services)

GVA Grimley

HOME PROPERTY SEARCH OCCUPIERS DEVELOPERS INVESTORS PUBLIC SECTOR
About Us Contact Us Research Press Office Careers Our Projects Sustainability

GVA Grimley puts satellite earth station up for sale
03/06/2005

GVA Grimley has been instructed to dispose of a very unusual Satellite Earth Station near Rugby.

To be sold as a complete business, the station receives and transmits signals to satellites, in order to provide internet traffic to areas where there are no existing fibre optic cables such as off-shore oil rigs, areas of North Africa and the former Eastern block. It is likely to be acquired by a satellite operator as a going concern.

David Speight, Head of Plant & Machinery at GVA Grimley comments, "This is one of the most unusual and interesting opportunities that we have come across. The property comprises two office buildings set in landscaped grounds and there is a considerable amount of recently installed, and well maintained, plant and machinery. One of the buildings is a former bunker, used as a regional seat of government during the Cold War, so the site also has an interesting history."

The station is located at Lawford Heath, approximately 2 miles west of Rugby, 6 miles east of Coventry and 25 miles east of Birmingham. The property comprises two office buildings, totalling approximately 8,113 sq ft, set in 5.8 acres of secure landscaped grounds with an ornamental pond and 24 car parking spaces.

GVA Grimley has been instructed by DJ Whitehouse and S Wilson, joint administrators of Teleport UK Ltd, trading as Satellite Media Services. The Satellite Earth Station will be sold by public tender and documents are required by 12 noon on Wednesday 15 June.

Publicity regarding the sale of former ROC 8 Group Control at Lawford Heath
(Soutrce: GVA Grimley Website, 2005)

Name:	LEEDS (18 Group)
Location:	Yeadon, Leeds
OS Grid Reference:	SE21904150
Operational Period:	1964 – 1968

The semi-sunk building replaced the former Group Control building which was based at Grove House in Hyde Park and was operational through the latter part of WW2 and was one of the last of the Group Control buildings to be built. The site was officially opened on the 11th April 1964 at a site at Yeadon to the North of Leeds and on the west side of the A658 Victoria Avenue just to the west of the current Leeds Bradford Airport.

Consisting of a three level semi-sunk building the building only provided four years service as a Group Control. As a result of the 1968 ROC structure reorganisation; 18 Group was disbanded and the Leeds bunker, now surplus to requirements, was closed. Also closed during this reorganisation were approximately half of those posts previously under the control of the Leeds Control. Within South Yorkshire all the smaller ROC Monitoring Posts would have been controlled from this Group Control, before being split after the building closed between the remaining Group Controls at Lincoln, York and Coventry.

After closure the bunker was taken over by the Royal Naval Reserve and used as a training facility. The Navy vacated the site in 1995 and the bunker was incorporated into an industrial estate. It is now in a secure car storage compound which is private property and is not accessible.

Leeds ROC - 18 Group Control in 2009
(Source: Noel J Ryan)

Leeds ROC - 18 Group Control on 21st January 1999
(Source: John Gedge via ROC Museum)

Name:	**LINCOLN (15 Group)**
Location:	**Fiskerton, Lincolnshire**
OS Grid Reference:	**TF04607250**
Operational Period:	**1960 – 1992**

The Lincoln 15 Group Control building is a semi-sunk design and is located on the site of the former RAF Fiskerton in the village of Fiskerton, approximately 7 kilometres east of Lincoln.

The site was one of the first of the "new" semi-sunk Group Controls to be operational from 10th December 1960. Having been left idle from the stand-down of the ROC in 1992; in 1998 the site was acquired by specialist ammunitions manufacturer "Primetake" who now uses the main plotting area of the bunker of the site for police training purposes[34].

Lincoln ROC - 15 Group Control on 30 June 1987
(Source: John Gadge via ROC Museum)

---

[34] Pictures of the inside of this site may be found on the Subterranea Britannica website (http://www.subbrit.org.uk/rsg/sites/f/fiskerton/)

Lincoln ROC - 15 Group Control in 1992
(Source: David Langlands / Charles Parker)

Main Table c.1960
(Source: ROC / Charles Parker)

Nuclear fallout being monitored during an exercise in late 1970s
(Source: ROC / Charles Parker)

Command table and vertical displays c.1973
(Source: David Langlands / Charles Parker)

Nuclear burst tote and displays c.1987
(Source: Charles Parker)

Tape Centre - Printing reperforators and teleprinter operator positions prior to full computerisation c.1987
(Source: Charles Parker)

Long range board c.1960
(Source: ROC / Charles Parker)

Triangulation Team at the table plotting GZI reports c.1979
(Source: David Langlands via Charles Parker)

Tape Centre supervisors collecting message tape c.1979
(Source: David Langlands via Charles Parker)

Name:	YORK (20 Group)
Location:	Acomb, York
OS Grid Reference:	SE 58065155
Operational Period:	1961 – 1991

The semi sunk York bunker was opened on the 16th December 1961 at a site to the rear of the former Shelley House and located on the north side of Acomb Road on the B1224 running west out of York.

A building was in keeping with other protected HQs and replaced the former Group Control building at Knavesmire (see above).

The HQ was modified in the late 1970s to early 1980s with the removal of part of the earth banking for the addition of a telescopic radio mast adjacent to the main entrance (compare the pictures below with that of Leeds above) and the replacement of the emergency exit ladder shaft at the south western end of the building with a flight of stairs.

The bunker was decommissioned in 1991 with the signing of a non-aggression treaty between NATO and the Warsaw Pact countries before being acquired by English Heritage.

The site underwent a £240,000 restoration programme by English Heritage and in 2006 the building was opened as a tourist attraction.

York ROC 20 Group Control - W/Observer Anne Wilde of 20/Crew 3 operating perforated paper tape unit.
(Source: MOD Photo 1248/11 via ROC Museum)

York ROC 20 Group Control - Observer Tony Calvert plotting bomb bursts
(Source: MOD Photo 1248/29 via ROC Museum)

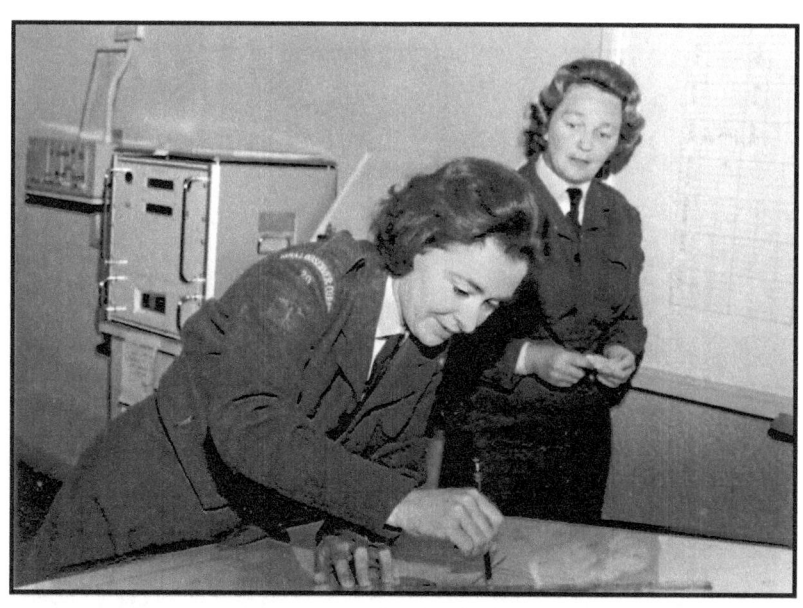

*York ROC 20 Group Control - Triangulation Team at work
(Left: W/Observer Ella Gibson 20/Crew 3 and Right: W/Observer Doreen
Angus 20/Crew 3)*
(Source: MOD Photo 1248/21 via ROC Museum)

*York ROC 20 Group Control - W/Observer Anne Wilde 20/Crew 3
operating a teleprinter.*
(Source: MOD Photo 1248/33 via ROC Museum)

York ROC 20 Group Control in Autumn 1991
(Source: John Gedge via ROC Museum)

York ROC 20 Group Control on 23rd November 1991
(Source: John Gedge via ROC Museum)

York ROC - 20 Group Control in 2009 (Above & Below)
(Source: Noel J Ryan)

York ROC - 20 Group Control in 2009 (Above & Below)
(Source: Noel J Ryan)

Plotting area of Group Control during a NATO exercise
(Source: SY ROC Museum)

Example of reporting tote balcony common to all sites – This was at 10 Group Control Exeter
(Source: Lawrence Holmes Collection)

Plotting Area
(Source: Mark Johnson Collection)

'A' & 'B' Plotting Boards
(Source: Chris Howells Collection) [www.chrishowells.co.uk]

Rotating Tote Boards
(Source: Chris Howells Collection) [www.chrishowells.co.uk]

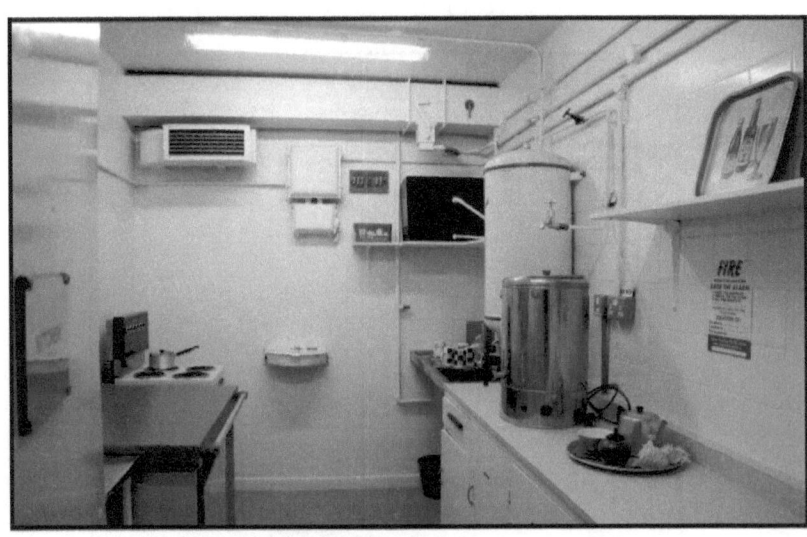

Control Kitchen
(Source: Chris Howells Collection) [www.chrishowells.co.uk]

R.O.C. MONITORING POSTS

General Locations

South Yorkshire had a total of ten ROC underground Monitoring Posts.

These were located at;

1. Askern, Doncaster
2. Beauchief, Sheffield
3. Darton, Barnsley
4. Ecclesfield / Hoyland, Rotherham
5. Goldthorpe, Barnsley
6. Lindholme, Doncaster
7. Rossington, Doncaster
8. Stocksbridge, Sheffield
9. Thorne, Doncaster
10. Wickersley, Rotherham

A further three posts were located outside the county but were linked into the South Yorkshire area through ROC communication clusters during the operational period. These include;

11. Blyth, Nottinghamshire
12. Buxton, Derbyshire
13. Whitwell, Nottinghamshire

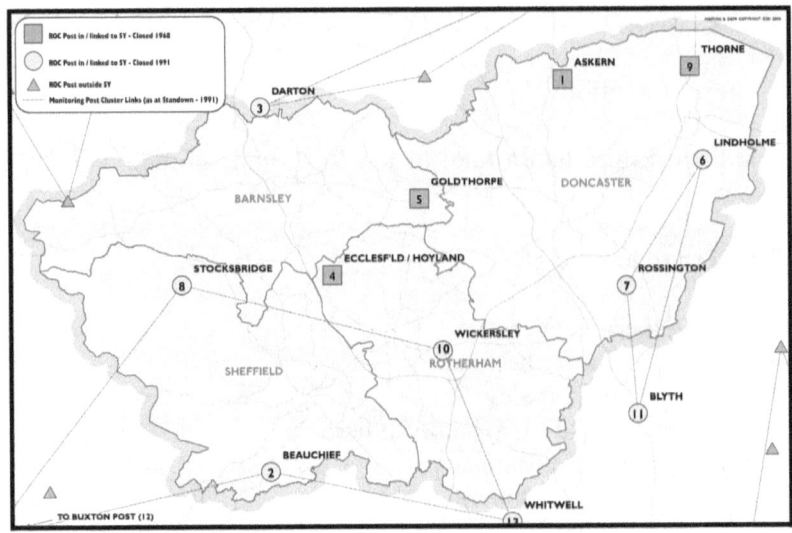

Four of these; Askern, Ecclesfield / Hoyland, Goldthorpe and Thorne were victims of the 1968 reorganisation and were subsequently closed, whilst the other six continued in use until 1991. Two of these were master posts which would have provided VHF radio contact through to group control. These posts are identifiable by the VHF radio dome on the side of the ventilation shaft.

Site Description and Plans

The ROC Monitoring Post was conceived in 1956 by the successful trial of a post at Farnham. Over the next decade a further 1559 posts were built around the country and formed into groups of between two and four and at approximately eight to ten miles apart from each other. The Monitoring Post is a concrete box measuring 4.75 metres long and 2.25 metres in length and height. The walls are built of reinforced concrete, which was believed to be capable of withstanding the blast effects of a nuclear device.

The construction of East Ham Underground Monitoring Post c.1959
(Source: SY ROC Museum)

The Post is buried approximately 4 metres in the ground and covered with earth to provide added protection from a nuclear blast. Access to the post is via a small pagoda hatch and down a shaft via a 3 metre long ladder leading into the small entrance shaft area of the post. Opposite the entrance area is the toilet area which consists of a small portable "Elsan" chemical toilet. The main monitoring area consists of a bunk bed, cupboard and monitoring table which allows easy reading of the monitoring equipment.

The main equipment used within these posts includes;

- Bomb Power Indicator (BPI) [mounted on Wall]
- Teletalk (AD8010) [for communication with Group Control]
- Fixed Survey Meter (FSM) [for assessing the level of radiation outside the post – linked via a wire to an ionisation probe located in the ceiling of the post]

- Ground Zero Indicator (GZI) [for assessing the magnitude of the bomb burst, location and whether ground burst or air burst].

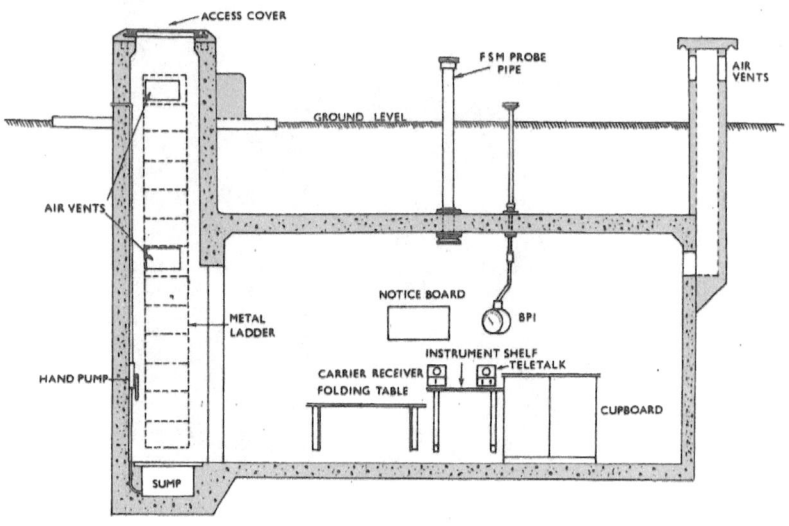

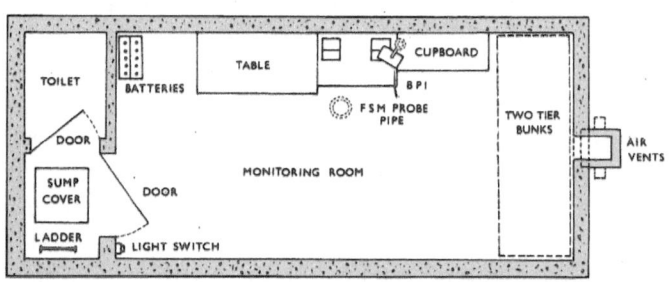

Plan of ROC Underground Monitoring Post
(Source: Wood, D.: Attack Warning Red – 1976)

Site Locations in South Yorkshire

Name:	ASKERN
Location:	Doncaster District
OS Grid Reference:	SE57331445
Operational Period:	1961 – 1968

The Askern ROC post was located to the northeast of Askern village, off Fenwick Lane to the north of Moss Road. The post was opened in 1961 and became a casualty of the 1968 reorganisation, closing that year. The post was soon afterwards demolished and today no trace remains.

Askern post. Now just a field, no evidence of a post ever being here
(Source: Noel J Ryan)

Name:	**BEAUCHIEF**
Location:	**Sheffield District**
OS Grid Reference:	**SK32618126**
Operational Period:	**1959 – 1991**

Beauchief ROC post was opened in 1959 and survived the 1968 reorganisation until eventual closure in September 1991 as a result of the ROC operational stand-down. The post is located in the overflow car park of the Abbeydale Golf Club and on the west side of a public footpath leading around Beauchief Hall. The entrance shaft, ventilation shaft with the ground zero mount, the fixed survey meter and the bomb power indicator can all be seen. The actual compound retains its integrity and the original gate to it is still in place.

With its position being so close to Sheffield the survivability of this post must be brought into question. Being an important industrial site, Sheffield would have been the target for multiple missiles and or bombs, obliterating the surrounding area for many miles. Permission was granted for the post to be "restored", however repeated break-ins and vandalism culminating in the post being set on fire made such a task uneconomic to achieve.

Beauchief Post. Entrance cupola
(Source: Noel J Ryan)

Entrance cupola with ground zero indicator mount visible to the right and fixed survey probe pipe to the left (Source: Noel J Ryan)

Ventilation shaft with non-original weather vane (Source: Noel J Ryan)

Original Entrance Gate
(Source: Noel J Ryan)

Name:	DARTON
Location:	Barnsley District
OS Grid Reference:	SE31891211
Operational Period:	1964 - 1991

The Darton post can be found off Gypsey Lane which itself runs off Woolley Edge Lane, adjacent to the former Woolley Colliery. A public footpath from Gypsey Lane leads part way to the post which is located on private farm land and thereby requiring permission to enter. The ventilation shaft is still visible but again slightly damaged. In between this and the entrance hatch the distinctive Fixed Survey Meter Probe pipe is evident. Darton was a master post identifiable by the VHF radio dome on the side of the ventilation shaft.

The post was opened in May 1964 and closed in September 1991. The entrance cupola has been damaged and the cover is missing, the ladder leading down into the bunker is still bolted to the shaft although access should not be attempted.

Darton ROC post remain.
(Source: Noel J Ryan)

Darton ROC post: The ventilation shaft and the mount for the Fixed Survey Meter Probe are visible.
(Source: Noel J Ryan)

Darton Post. The VHF radio dome signifying that this was a master post.
(Source: Noel J Ryan)

Name:	ECCLESFIELD / HOYLAND
Location:	Rotherham District
OS Grid Reference:	SK37909790
Operational Period:	1965 - 1968

Rather strangely this post, originally named Ecclesfield (after the original overground post which it replaced) and being renamed Hoyland in January 1966, was at neither location. It was actually just outside the small village of Wentworth, at the junction of Churchfield Lane and Ashes Lane.

Whatever name it went by it was to have a short career, opening in April 1965 it failed to survive the reorganisation of 1968 closing in October of that year. The post was demolished by the farmer of the land on which it was located. The only evidence of its existence being the former access gate by the road.

Ecclesfield / Hoyland post. Only the former gate remains.
(Source: Noel J Ryan)

Name:	GOLDTHORPE
Location:	Barnsley District
OS Grid Reference:	SE45240437
Operational Period:	1961 – 1968

The Goldthorpe ROC post has been completely lost to redevelopment with no trace of anything remaining. Its location was between Barnsley Road and the new Goldthorpe by-pass, the A635. The site was cleared during construction of the by-pass and later was covered by new housing.

The post was another relatively short-lived one. Opening in May 1961 and closing in October 1968.

Goldthorpe post. The post was totally demolished and the location is now occupied by new housing.
(Source: Noel J Ryan)

Name:	**LINDHOLME**
Location:	**Doncaster District**
OS Grid Reference:	**SE69060757**
Operational Period:	**1962 – 1991**

Lindholme ROC post is located off Moor Dyke Road which can be accessed from the south of Hatfield. The post is just off the northern perimeter track of the former RAF Lindholme airfield. This is now Home Office property with two prisons on site.

The post was opened in May 1962 and survived until the nuclear monitoring role was wound up, closing in September 1991. Today the entrance cupola, ventilation shaft cover and the Bomb Power Indicator mount can still be seen with the post being in good condition. In 2010 the post was offered for sale by its owned having acquired it a few years earlier.

Obs. John Fletcher opening the post for Exercise INTEX 1974
(Source: Charles Parker)

Lindholme Post. Entrance hatch.
(Source: Noel J Ryan)

Lindholme Post. Fixed Survey Meter Probe Cover mount.
(Source: Noel J Ryan)

Lindholme Post. Ventilation shaft.
(Source: Noel J Ryan)

Name:	ROSSINGTON
Location:	Doncaster District
OS Grid Reference:	SK62589695
Operational Period:	1963 – 1991

Rossington ROC post can still be seen today located in a fenced compound at the junction of Stripe Road and Common Lane, just south of Rossington village. Rossington was a master post identifiable by a aerial connections dome on the ventilation shaft *(refer to Blyth Post reference for picture)*. Opened in May 1963 it saw almost 30 years service, closing in September 1991.

Since closure the site has been extensively vandalised with the entrance hatch now permanently removed and the inside suffering severe fire damage. All surface features remain although the ventilation shaft is damaged. Access should not be attempted, as well as being dangerous the post is owned privately.

Rossington post. The water tower in the background is a good point of reference for the post location.
(Source: Noel J Ryan)

Two views of the entrance hatch.
(Source: Noel J Ryan) (Both)

Some internal photos are included showing the burnt out state of the interior.

Looking down the entrance shaft.
(Source: Noel J Ryan)

Rossington post. Looking back up the entrance shaft. Note remains of counter-balance on the right.
(Source: Jeremy Wickens)

Two interior photos showing the current burnt out state. Note the cupboard and pump handle.
(Source: Jeremy Wickens)

Name:	STOCKSBRIDGE
Location:	Sheffield District
OS Grid Reference:	SK25249708
Operational Period:	1964 – 1991

Situated on high ground to the south of Stocksbridge off Heads Lane, this post would have been ideally placed to witness the destruction of Sheffield. Opening in January 1964 it continued in service until closure in September 1991. Shortly after stand-down of the Royal Observer Corps in 1991, all surface features were demolished and no trace of the post exists except for a mound in a field.

Name:	THORNE
Location:	Doncaster District
OS Grid Reference:	SE68001550
Operational Period:	1962 – 1968

The Thorne post was sited to the north of Thorne, south of North Common Road which runs east off the A614. The post opened in May 1962 and was closed in October 1968. Nothing of the actual post remains today and the location is hard to establish. There is an abandoned wooden access gate along the side of the road which was probably the former access.

Thorne post. Believed to be the former access gate. All other traces of this post have gone.

(Source: Noel J Ryan)

Name:	**WICKERSLEY**
Location:	**Rotherham District**
OS Grid Reference:	**SK47149149**
Operational Period:	**1963 - 1991**

The Wickersley post was situated in the rear garden of Bracken Lodge on the west side of Hollin Moor Lane off the A631 Bawtry Road. The underground post was opened in 1963 and was operational until September 1991 when the post was passed back to the landowner. In 1993 the post was demolished and the site was reincorporated back into the rear garden of Bracken Lodge.

Although today nothing remains of this post, much of the equipment used within this post was donated to the South Yorkshire ROC Museum located at the South Yorkshire Aircraft Museum (AeroVenture) for permanent display.

External view of Wickersley post during operations in the 80s

(Source: SYROCM Collection)

Internal view of Wickersley post during operations in the 80s

(Source: SYROCM Collection)

Site Locations outside South Yorkshire

Name:	BLYTH
Location:	Nottinghamshire
OS Grid Reference:	SK63488609
Operational Period:	1964 - 1991

Blyth post is located in a square compound on the South side of Long Brecks Lane close to overhead power lines. The hatch is open and like a number of posts where access is possible, it has been badly damaged by fire. Some of the wiring and kitchen utensils remain together with the folding table, shelf, cupboard, a single bed and two chairs.

The open entrance hatch of Blyth Post
(Source: Noel J Ryan)

Looking down the access hatch (above) and ventilation chimney (below)
(Source: Noel J Ryan)

Name:	BUXTON
Location:	Derbyshire
OS Grid Reference:	SK08777564
Operational Period:	1959 - 1991

Buxton post is located on a hilltop 150 yards east of Longridge Lane and north of the track to Broadlow Farm. The post is in reasonably good condition and has been well maintained. The post was initially sold in 2003 and was surveyed by members of the Subterranea Britannica group in that year.

By 2008, however the post had undergone a refurbishment and again found itself up for sale by auction; this time on the internet auction site Ebay, with a starting price of £18,000.

Buxton Post taken in 2008 after refurbishment (above and below)
(Source: Noel J Ryan)

Name:	WHITWELL
Location:	Nottinghamshire
OS Grid Reference:	SK52937695
Operational Period:	1959 - 1991

Whitwell post is located in an overgrown square compound at the end of a line of telegraph poles 50 yards west of the B6043 road. The last telegraph pole in the line is an unusual metal one with a circular plate on the top. All surface features remain intact with the green paint flaking badly. There are two steps, one on either side of the access shaft which was rebuilt in 1989 and a new larger entrance hatch (Torlift) fitted.

Many of the instruments used within the Whitwell post (as well as other local posts) were donated to the South Yorkshire ROC Museum located within the South Yorkshire Aircraft Museum (Aeroventure) and are on permanent display. The hatch was welded shut by the landowner in order to reduce the risk of accidents.

Whitwell Post showing the "non-standard" steel telegraph pole
(Source: Noel J Ryan)

Whitwell Post showing the Torlift Hatch entrance and ventilation "chimney" (Source: Noel J Ryan)

R.O.C. NUCLEAR REPORTING CELL

Name:	BAWTRY HALL / RAF BAWTRY
Location:	South Yorkshire
OS Grid Reference:	SK65079298

Bawtry Hall is in the village of Bawtry just South of Doncaster. The site became the HQ of 1 Group Bomber Command in July 1941. 1 Group was to remain at Bawtry as an RAF command group well into the cold war years, controlling the V force and other units, before moving to RAF Waddington.

During the later stages of the Cold War, Bawtry Hall became Strike Command HQ and in 1982 became famous for co-ordinating the bombing of the airfield at Port Stanley by Vulcan bombers from RAF Finningley during the Falklands conflict from the operations room at Bawtry Hall. For a while, RAF Bawtry continued to function as the centre of the RAF meteorological service until in January 1984; HQ One Group was moved to RAF Upavon in Wiltshire and the RAF finally vacated Bawtry Hall. The group still exists today as an Air Combat Group containing all fast jet assets including the Joint Force Harrier (JFH), formerly part of No 3 Group, and the Joint Force Air Component (JFAC) HQ, which is currently a centrally provided asset.

Today Bawtry Hall is a retreat and conference centre. Some of the RAF buildings still stand and a memorial is built into one of the walls of what was the post WW2 command room, the original WW2 operations is now known as the Peake room..

Building consisting of the post WW2 command room showing memorial.
(Source: Noel J Ryan)

CHAPTER 10

UTILITY & OTHER ORGANISATIONS CONTROLLED SITES

WATER

Name:	LANGSETT WATER TREATMENT WORKS
Location:	Langsett, Sheffield, South Yorkshire
OS Grid Reference:	-----------

The Yorkshire Water Emergency Control is located at the Langsett Water Treatment Works which is located to the north of Sheffield next to the district boundary between Sheffield and Barnsley. It is believed that the site is one of ten such sites built by Yorkshire Water during the mid 1980s to a Swiss Civil Defence form and consists of a protected underground structure which covers a footprint of approximately 10m x 25m[35].

The bunker consists of a number of airtight blast-proof doors which lead into the first of two main rooms. The first room would have been the main living area and would have access into the toilets and kitchen area. The bunker would have enabled water engineers to live comfortably for a minimum of two weeks. Access from this main room may be gained into a second main room which would have been the main operations room to the building. Access may be further gained through to the generator room and escape tunnels.

---

[35] These figures are estimates based on measurements taken from aerial imagery.

The surface building leading into the Yorkshire Water Langsett Water Bunker (Above & Below)
(Source: Noel J Ryan)

Name:	DONCASTER
Location:	South Yorkshire
OS Grid Reference:	Unknown
Operational Period:	Unknown

It is believed that during the 1980s, Yorkshire Water Authority constructed 10 emergency control structures within their region. Two of these structures were deemed to be located in South Yorkshire; Langsett (see above) and Doncaster. It is not known whether an actual protected building was built in Doncaster and its exact whereabouts[36].

ELECTRICITY

Name:	BECCA HALL & ROTHWELL HAIGH
Location:	Aberford & Rothwell, Nr Leeds
OS Grid Reference:	SE41883888 & SE32452755
Operational Period:	1950s – 1990s

Blast proof accommodation was provided for the electricity industry in the early 1950s. In 1950 it was felt necessary to provide dispersed national and regional control centres. The Main National Grid control centre (including Atomic and Computer Centre) was located at Becca Hall while a smaller site located at Rothwell Haigh to the South of Leeds acted as a regional control centre / standby control. The rooms were manned by Control Engineers, who worked round-the-clock shifts and were responsible for the operations for the cost-effective management & supply of electricity generation to the main interconnected system network (132 / 275 & 400kV). They also held details of both the running costs and availability of every power plant in England and Wales.

At these control centres they would continuously predict demand and supervise, directing power stations to either increase or reduce production, or to cease production altogether. They used what was known as the 'merit order' — a method used to rank each generator

---

[36] The authors would welcome any information regarding the possible existence of such a site in / around Doncaster.

in the power stations based on how much each cost to produce electricity. The idea was to make sure that production was always achieved at the lowest possible cost.

Becca Hall

Becca Hall is located at Aberford to the East of Leeds and for most of the 20th century was owned by the Central Electricity Generating Board (CEGB). Following on from the privatisation of the UK Electricity in 1989; the introduction of the Central Electricity Generating Board (Dissolution) Order 2001, which formed a Statutory Instrument through Parliament, led to the eventual break-up of the CEGB. The order came into effect on the 9 November 2001. This ultimately created out of the former CEGB, two main generating companies; National Power & Powergen, and the National Grid Company whose aims were to manage the miles of cables, pylons and other electrical systems as part of the electricity national grid. As a result Becca Hall passed along to this new organisation.

Behind the main house, there existed a purposely built Grid Control Centre for the UK's electricity transmission network which constructed in 1958; was operational until 1997. As developments in communication progressed including the increased ability and effectiveness of remote operations; the need for regional control centres was reduced. By the time of its operational closure in 1997, England and Wales' entire electricity transmission network could be controlled from a single control room anywhere in the country. Later in its use it is believed to have been used as a control centre for the Dinorwig hydroelectric Stored Energy Power Station in North Wales.

The latter National Grid sign on the wall of Becca Hall
(Source: Noel J. Ryan)

Becca Hall on the left with the Control Centre to the right
(Source: Noel J. Ryan)

Becca Hall control centre from the front
(Source: Noel J. Ryan)

Becca Hall control centre from the side showing the security turnstiles for access to the building
(Source: Noel J. Ryan)

Security turnstiles for access to the building
(Source: Noel J. Ryan)

Rothwell Haigh

The CEGB Leeds regional control centre was built in 1953 and was one of two such "bunkers" in the small Leeds hamlet of Rothwell. It was located alongside a larger GPO/BT 'PR2' repeater station which was located at the corner of Sharp Lane and the A61. The building is approximately 30m long and 8m wide, and along with the GPO repeater station formed a small emergency complex along with nearby buildings forming RAF Rothwell Haigh.

The site was disposed of in the mid 1990s and is now a commercial construction business.

The surface building of the former CEGB Bunker
(Source: Mark Johnson Collection)

TELECOM

Name:	ROTHWELL HAIGH
Location:	Rothwell, Nr Leeds
OS Grid Reference:	SE32502760

The main purpose of the repeater station is to maintain the effective transfer of a telephone call along a line by amplifying the signal at regular intervals in order to maintain its strength from one point to another. In early days of telephony, all telephone traffic was carried over copper conductors in telephone cables.

Copper wire although being a relatively good conductor of electricity; attenuates signals sent over a long length of cable (approximately 30km). The signal level then reduces, such that the electrical noise on the line can swamp the signal altogether. The required amplification required cannot be provided simply at either the sending end or receiving end of the line (although most large Automatic Telephone Exchange buildings did incorporate a repeater station).The repeater stations therefore provide the required amplification of the telephone signal at a number of points along the line. The site at Rothwell Haigh was an especially hardened repeaters station capable of withstanding a nuclear blast. The site which housed a switching centre for the buildings of RAF Rothwell Haigh was cleared during 2008/9 to make way for new housing developments.

OTHER BUILDINGS / SITES OF RELEVANCE

Banking

Name:	HSBC (formerly Midland Bank) South Yorkshire National Data Centre
Location:	Tankersley, Nr Barnsley, South Yorkshire
OS Grid Reference:	SK33829928
Operational Period:	1981 - Present

During the 1970s, Midland Bank Ltd took the decision to decentralise many of its head office support functions from London to Sheffield. Midland Bank recognised that the storage of its computer data was paramount and any loss of such data would potentially lead to a serious impact upon the operations of the Bank or ultimately its demise. As a result the bank commissioned the construction of a secure data centre which aimed to safely manage and store the increasing wealth of account details and information, important to Midland Bank's everyday operations.

The site was designed to withstand the blast and effect of a nuclear bomb or a direct hit by a plane is located less than a kilometre from the M1 Junction 36 and was finally completed in 1981 at a cost of approximately £40 million. The site was designed in two halves each mirroring the other and separated by the main operations building known to some as "The Bridge" (see photo below) and provides a 24 hour a day; 365 days a year, operation with full contingency against system problems.

In 1992 Midland Bank became a principal member of the HSBC Group which started life as the Hong Kong and Shanghai Banking Corporation Limited in 1865 to finance the growing trade between China and Europe.

HSBC's South Yorkshire National Data Centre
(Source: Noel J Ryan)

HSBC's South Yorkshire National Data Centre – Control Room known to some as "The Bridge"
(Source: Noel J Ryan)

RAF Missile Protection

Name:	RAF Lindholme Tactical Control Centre (TCC)
Location:	Lindholme, Nr Doncaster South Yorkshire
OS Grid Reference:	SE67650685
Operational Period:	1953 – 1963

The threat during the Cold War no longer came from low flying aircraft that had been common throughout the Cold War, but ultimately came from high altitude strategic bombers such as the Tupolev Tu-95 (NATO Codename – "Bear") carrying nuclear weapons. Since WW2; missile technology developed considerably as propulsion technology and guidance systems improved. Such missiles focused towards delivering nuclear and conventional warheads.

During the early 1950s a new system of defence was developed to counter this threat from the Soviet Union and was based on a series of Surface to Air Guided Missiles (SAMs) known as "Bloodhound". Initially proposed for placement at adapted Anti-Aircraft sites the move towards high altitude bombers necessitated the construction of larger missile sites to enable multiple missiles ("fire-units") to intercept bombers before reaching the UK coast. In total; eleven sites were developed;

- RAF Breighton, East Riding (NGR: SE72023501)
- RAF Carnaby, North Yorks (NGR:TA13546387)
- RAF Dunholme Lodge, Lincs (NGR: SK99697819)
- RAF Marham, Norfolk (NGR: TF73310829)
- RAF Misson, Notts (NGR: SK70349741)
- RAF North Coates, Lincs (NGR: TA37090221)
- RAF Rattlesden, Suffolk (NGR:TL96505640)
- RAF Warboys, Cambs (NGR:TL29367873)
- RAF Watton, Norfolk (NGR: TF94179993)
- RAF Woodhall Spa, Lincs (NGR: TF20996113)
- RAF Woodfox Lodge, Rutland (NGR: SK96151333)

In order to target and fire the Bloodhound Mk1 missiles, these ten sites relied on tracking information gathered from one of four Tactical Control Centres (TCC) located at;

- **RAF Lindholme, South Yorks (NGR: SE67650685)**
- RAF North Cotes, Lincs (NGR: TA37090221)
- RAF North Luffenham, Rutland (NGR:SK96151333)
- RAF Watton, Norfolk (NGR: TF94179993)

The table below shows the TCCs which controlled the main missile sites.

TCC SITE	MISSILE SITE
RAF Lindholme	RAF Breighton RAF Carnaby RAF Misson
RAF North Coates	RAFDunholme Lodge RAF North Coates RAF Woodhall Spa
RAF North Luffenham	RAF Warboys RAF Woolfox Lodge
RAF Watton	RAF Marham RAF Rattlesden RAF Watton

The TCC's were assisted by their own radar and forwarded launch information through to the semi-mobile Launch Control Posts located at the missile sites which further utilised their own radar to guide the decision when the missiles were to be launched. The TCCs received the warning of potential attack directly from the Early Warning Radar system located at sites such as Staxton Wold / Patrington (Yorkshire); Trimmingham / Neatishead (Norfolk) or Bawdsey (Suffolk) and which formed the main receiver of information regarding a potential enemy attack.

The introduction of the Bloodhound Mk II missiles in the early 1960's meant that a separate TCC building was not required. The initial threat was still identified and sent from the Early Warning Radar system with basic radar co-ordinates being forwarded directly to the Bloodhound Launch Control Post and associated

Target Illuminating Radars rather than via the TCC building. This led to the Lindholme TCC site becoming redundant.

Later in the 1970s / 80s the site became Northern Radar, which was one of a number of Joint Air Traffic Control Units (JATCRU) around the UK whose civil task were to provide area radar cover for the then three area Air Traffic Control Centres (ATCCs) at Prestwick (Scotland); Barton Hall Nr Preston, and at West Drayton near London. JATCRUs were created to provide this area radar cover as the ATCCs did not have radar facilities and were purely procedural control centres. The JATCRUs were located at RAF units using a mixture of civilian and military staff and radio communications but using the military radar systems.[37]

RAF Lindholme: Former Tactical Control Centre / Northern Radar (JATCRU) in 2007
(Source: Chris Percy)

---

[37] Information sources from Wikipedia.

RAF Lindholme: The remaining tower (minus radar apparatus) for the Type 82 Radar "Orange Yeoman" system
(Source: Chris Percy)

SECTION 5
FURTHER RESEARCH

KEY SITES FOR RESEARCH & VISITS

The following are sites and museums which are open to the public for visiting and further research purposes. The website of the site / museum is included, and should be the first "port-of-call" for further information of the site including visiting.

Wherever possible the authors have tried to include as many as possible of interesting and informative sites, however for any sites excluded the authors offer their apologies, and please feel free to contact the authors who would be happy to incorporate any other sites within any further editions.

Sites

English Heritage – ROC 20 Group Control - York

The York Cold War Bunker is a two-storey semi-sunk former Royal Observer Corps Group Control building (See Chapter 9). The site was opened to the public in 2006 by English Heritage as a tourist attraction. The site is only accessible by tour.

WEB: www.english-heritage.org.uk

Hack Green Secret Bunker – Hack Green, Cheshire

Hack Green Secret Bunker is located in the heart of the Cheshire countryside, a few miles outside the picturesque market town of Nantwich, and only 30 minutes from Chester. The semi-sunken site consists of two floors which include an extensive range of exhibits relating to the Cold War, military and nuclear technology, radar and the Royal Observer Corps.

WEB: www.hackgreen.co.uk

Kelvedon Hatch Secret Bunker – Kelvedon Hatch, Essex

The Bunker is located at Kelvedon Hatch, Essex and consists of three levels totally underground and accessed through a site bungalow and 150ft tunnel. The site initially started life as an RAF ROTOR Station before becoming briefly a civil defence centre during the 1960s. Latterly it became a Regional Government Headquarters. There are many exhibits within the site which include;

- The initial ground floor level consists of the main communication, military, and plant equipment
- The Second Level is the government level and explains the role of Government in time of Nuclear Attack.
- The top level of the bunker deals with the day to day existence of the bunkers inhabitants and includes a small surgery; several washrooms, dormitories, and a canteen.

WEB: www.secretnuclearbunker.com

Newark Air Museum – Newark, Nottinghamshire

The Newark Air Museum is located on part of the former World War Two airfield of Winthorpe in eastern Nottinghamshire. The museum features an expanding collection of well looked after exhibits, including a number of unique or significant airframes. All are maintained in good condition.

Access can be gained to the interior of the Hastings and Shackleton for modest fee. There is an extensive under-cover display area incorporating an extensive range of aviation artefacts and aviation memorabilia including:

- The Lancaster Corner
- Missiles & avionic systems
- Aerial Photography

- The Royal Institute of Navigation's 'Timeline' display and associated navigation equipment.
- The History of the Air Engineer
- A diverse selection of aero engines

Newark also has quite a comprehensive ROC display with an almost full size mock up of an underground post and a large collection of radiac instruments, ROC badges and training items. The display includes the triangulation table and "AD9000" switchboard from Lincoln ROC 15 Group Control at Fiskerton and "AWDREY" computer.

WEB: www.newarkairmuseum.org

Newhaven Fort Museum – Newhaven, East Sussex

Newhaven Fort is an award-winning attraction and a fine example of an English fortification. The site recreates the sights, sounds - even the smells - of the period, all found in a range of exhibitions and audio-visual presentations. The scheduled ancient monument tells the story of life in a Victorian Fortress and the on-site military museum demonstrates Newhaven Fort's role through two World Wars including the role of the Royal Observer Corps in both the Second World War and Cold War. The museum is also home to the Royal Observer Corps Historic Collection.

WEB: www.newhavenfort.org.uk

Imperial War Museum Duxford – Cambridgeshire

The Imperial War Museum at Duxford houses many of the IWM's large exhibits including the aircraft and military and naval vehicles collection. The site houses seven main exhibition buildings with nearly 200 military and civil aircraft. Buildings, such as the control tower, operations room and hangars which were used in the 1940s as a military airfield have been maintained and restored along with the Operations Room which has been carefully reconstructed to look as it did when Royal Air Force (RAF) personnel directed Duxford's fighters during the Battle of Britain.

Duxford's American Air Museum contains Duxford's collection of American military aircraft from First World War biplanes to supersonic jets and is a memorial to the 30,000 US airmen who lost their lives flying from British bases during the Second World War. Duxford's Land Warfare Hall houses tanks, vehicles and artillery from the First World War through the Cold War to the Gulf War.

WEB: http://duxford.iwm.org.uk/

Imperial War Museum North – Trafford, Greater Manchester

The Imperial War Museum North is located at The Quays, Trafford Wharf. The museum focuses on individuals and their relation to wars, past and present and especially aiming to "tell the story of how war has shaped the lives of British and Commonwealth citizens since 1914". Its main exhibition space houses the "Big Picture Show", a collection of projected images and sounds that play every hour, on the hour. The museum also houses war machinery and hosts rotating exhibitions.

WEB: http://north.iwm.org.uk

Imperial War Museum London

The Imperial War Museum is located in Central London, and documents British and Commonwealth history since 1914. The Museum houses a wide range of collections on numerous levels including

- military vehicles and aircraft,
- weapons,
- war memorabilia,
- an extensive library and archive of personal and official papers,
- film and photographic archives,
- a large art collection and a sound archive of oral history interviews and other material.

WEB: www.iwm.org.uk

Norfolk & Suffolk Aviation Museum - Flixton, Suffolk

The Norfolk and Suffolk Aviation Museum is recognised as East Anglia's Aviation Heritage Centre. Maintained and run by volunteers, with one paid staff member, the Museum celebrated its 35th Anniversary in 2007. Constituting an impressive collection of aircraft and equipment, the Museum also displays in separate buildings themed collections for the Royal Observer Corps No. 6 Group, the 446th (H) Bomb Group USAAF, RAF Bomber Command, RAF Air-Sea Rescue & Coastal Command, and local aviation through the years. There are also numerous exhibitions on special subjects including WWII Decoy Crews, Boulton & Paul, RAF training aids, aerial photography, and the Home Front.

WEB: www.aviationmuseum.net

RAF Holmpton – Withernsea, East Riding

The present site of RAF Holmpton was built between 1951 and 1952 and started its operational life in 1953 as an Early Warning Radar Station. In February 2003 development started to gradually restore the whole site and initially provide a facility holding Archives and photographs of underground defence establishments built in the British Isles between 1945 and the present day.

The site now contains a wide range of exhibits including;

- RAF Support Command Centre
- 1960s Message Centre
- Royal Observer Corps Operations Room
- Coding & Encryption Centre
- 1970s Radar Operations Centre and

WEB: www.rafholmpton.com

Royal Air Force Museum Cosford & National Cold War Exhibition

The RAF Museum at Cosford houses 70 aircraft and is home to War Planes, Missiles, Transport & Training and Research & Development collections. The site also houses the "The National Cold War Exhibition" which incorporates a wide and varied coverage of the Cold War period utilising interactive kiosks and hotspots to give visitors a chance to see what life was like behind the Iron Curtain.

WEB: www.rafmuseum.org.uk/cosford
WEB: www.nationalcoldwarexhibition.org.uk

Royal Air Force Museum Hendon

The Royal Air Force Museum Hendon is located in North London. The site comprises five exhibition halls which house exhibits covering;

- Milestones of Flight
- The Bomber Hall
- Historic Hangars
- The Battle of Britain Hall
- The Grahame-White Factory

The site houses approximately 130 aircraft including the only two surviving Vickers Wellingtons (from "bouncing bomb fame") in the world and the Avro Lancaster. From the Cold War, It also includes the Avro Vulcan "V-Bomber" that would have played a major role during Cold War and assisted greatly during the Falkland conflict.

WEB: www.rafmuseum.org.uk/london

Royal Observer Corps Museum Trust - Hampshire

The Royal Observer Corps Museum is the National Museum of the ROC and has an unrivalled collection of photographs, documents, records, equipment, artefacts and memorabilia covering the history of the ROC from its formation in 1925 until final stand-down in 1995.

The ROC Museum was started by Officers at the Winchester ROC Centre (14 Group) as a Collection for viewing by visitors. As the Collection grew it was moved into the disused wartime Operations Room, opening for visitors in June 1974. The Museum was developed with the aid of grants by Hampshire County Council (HCC) and opened to the public on 24 October 1987. The building closed in March 1992 with the partial stand-down of the ROC and the bulk of the Collection was moved out.

Through the generosity of HCC the Collection is housed near Winchester in leased premises. Hampshire County Museums & Archives Service provides professional advice on both Curatorial and Conservation matters to the Museum. The ROC Archive is lodged in Hampshire Record Office where it has been made available for direct access by the public. The ROC film Archive is in the care of Wessex Film & Sound Archive Trust.

WEB: www.therocmuseum.org.uk

Scotlands Secret Bunker – Anstruther, Fife, Scotland

Scotland's Secret Bunker is located at Troywood Nr Anstruther in Fife, close to the key enemy targets of the Royal Navy's Rosyth dockyard and the fighter aircraft of RAF Leuchars. The site is hidden beneath an innocent Scottish Farmhouse and a tunnel leads to main bunker complex. The site offers the visitor the ability to discover the world of the Government Cold War machine and offer the opportunity to discover how they would have survived, and the general population generally wouldn't.

WEB: www.secretbunker.co.uk

South Yorkshire Aircraft Museum (incorporating the South Yorkshire Royal Observer Corps Collection), Doncaster

AeroVenture, South Yorkshire's air museum is located at Doncaster's Lakeside - the former site of WWII RAF Doncaster. The museum is a treasure trove of aviation history and as most of the exhibits are under cover, it is ideal for sunny or rainy days.

Features at the museum includes:-

- Military Aircraft collection from propeller training aircraft to Mach 2 Jet fighters
- Historic 60 year old RAF buildings including Bellman aircraft hangar and authentic wooden RAF huts
- Helicopter Collection
- Commercial Light Aircraft Collection
- Piston Engine Collection including Rolls Royce Merlin and Griffon
- Jet Engine Collection including DeHavilland Ghost, Rolls Royce Avon and Conway
- Sheffield Blitz Exhibition
- WWII Home Front Exhibition
- Local Airfields - then and now including RAF Doncaster, Finningley, Lindholme, Worksop and Firbeck
- Amateur Radio Society "GB2AIR"
- History of local RAF Squadrons including 616 (South Yorkshire) Squadron which fought in the Battle of Britain and were the first operational jet squadron and 271 Squadron which took part in D-Day flying Dakotas
- Falklands Exhibition

The site also contains the South Yorkshire Royal Observer Corps Museum, which is contained in a former RAF Vulcan Pilot dispersal building provides the history of the Royal Observer Corps from its start to the Corps stand-down in the 1990s. The ROC Museum contains many instruments as used by the ROC, ranging from the Portable Hand-Held Siren to radiation meters, plastic weapons effects calculators, Ground Zero Indicator and Bomb Power Indicator. WEB: www.aeroventure.org.uk

Royal Air Force Air Defence Radar Museum - RAF Neatishead - Norfolk

The RAF Defence Radar Museum is located at RAF Neatishead to the North of Norwich. In October 1994 the original operations building which housed the old equipment was converted into the Air Defence Radar Museum, and since then the museum has developed a range of exhibits relating to Radar.

The museum traces the history and development of Air Defence Radar since its invention in 1935 and incorporates exhibits relating to the history and development of Detection, Air Intelligence Photography, Air Defence Radar and Air Battle Management from the 1930s to the modern computer technology of today. The museum incorporates a ROC display along with a preserved Cold War Operations Room exactly as it would have been in 1954 and Bloodhound missile on its launcher.

The end of the cold war means that the secret world of air defence is open to public scrutiny. Thousands of items of memorabilia, accessible photo albums showing the pictorial history of RAF Neatishead are also all on public display.

WEB: www.radarmuseum.co.uk

BOOKS & DOCUMENTS

GENERAL RESEARCH

Buckton, H; 1993, Forewarned is Forearmed: An official tribute and history of the Royal Observer Corps. Leatherhead: Ashford, Buchan & Enwright

Campbell, D; 1983, War Plan UK. London: Paladin [Out-of-print but available through libraries]

Clarke, B; 2005, Four Minute Warning – Britain's Cold War. Stroud: Tempus Publishing

Cocroft, W D & Thomas, R J C; 2004, Cold War – Building for Nuclear Confrontation 1946 – 1989. Swindon: English Heritage

Fox, S; 2004, Struggle for Survival – Governing Britain after the Bomb. Available online at www.subbrit.org.uk

McCamley, N J; 2002, Cold War Secret Nuclear Bunkers. Barnsley: Pen & Sword

Parker C S; 1991. The Royal Observer Corps in Lincolnshire 1936-1991. Boston: Lincolnshire Aviation Society Ltd

Wood, D; 1991, Attack Warning Red: The Royal Observer Corps and the Defence of Britain 1925 – 1992 (2nd Edition). Portsmouth: Carmichael & Sweet

SOURCES RELATING TO THE BOOK CHAPTERS

Chapter 1

Marienfelde Refugee Centre Museum; 2006, Flight in Divided Germany. Erinnerungsstätte Notaufnahmelager Marienfelde e.V. Berlin

http://www.trumanlibrary.org [ONLINE]
http://library.thinkquest.org/11046/days/bay_of_pigs.html [ONLINE]
http://en.wikipedia.org/wiki/Cuban_Missile_Crisis [ONLINE]

Chapter 2

Campbell, D; 1983, War Plan UK. London: Paladin
Cocroft, W D & Thomas, R J C; 2004, Cold War – Building for Nuclear Confrontation 1946 – 1989. Swindon: English Heritage
Fox, S; 2004, Struggle for Survival – Governing Britain after the Bomb. [Available online at www.subbrit.org.uk]
Home Office; 1965, Police War Duties Manual: HMSO
Home Office; 1974, Nuclear Weapons (2nd Impression): HMSO
Home Office; 1981, Emergency Services Circular ES1/1981: HMSO
McCamley, N J; 2002, Cold War Secret Nuclear Bunkers. Barnsley: Pen & Sword
Openshaw, S et al; 1983, Doomsday – Britain after Nuclear Attack. Oxford: Basil Blackwell Publishers

http://www.fas.org/nuke/intro/nuke/radiation.htm [ONLINE]

Chapter 3

Wiltshire County Council; 1985, Wiltshire War Book: Wiltshire County Council

Chapter 4

Buckton, H; 1993, Forewarned is Forearmed: An official tribute and history of the Royal Observer Corps. Leatherhead: Ashford, Buchan & Enwright
Home Office; 1974, United Kingdom Warning & Monitoring Organisation. London: HMSO
Parker C S; 1991, The Royal Observer Corps In Lincolnshire 1936-1991. Boston: Lincolnshire Aviation Society Ltd
Spence, N; 1987, Watchers over the Broad Acres. Harrogate: John Ramsay Marketing Limited.

Winslow, T E; 1948, The Authorized History of the Royal Observer Corps. London: William Hodge & Company Limited

Wood, D; 1976, Attack Warning Red: The Royal Observer Corps and the Defence of Britain 1925 – 1992 (1st Edition). Portsmouth: Carmichael & Sweet

Chapter 5

Hand, G R; 2003, In Time of War or Crisis – The Green Goddess Story. Sheffield: Sheffield Fire & Police Museum

http://www.brindale.co.uk/ach/prv_site/external_links/green_goddess_article.htm

Chapter 6

Campbell, D; 1983, War Plan UK. London: Paladin

Kent County Council; 1986, Community Volunteer Training Handbook. Maidstone: Kent County Council Emergency Planning Dept.

Chapter 7

Campbell, D; 1983, War Plan UK. London: Paladin

Clarke, B; 2005, Four Minute Warning – Britain's Cold War. Stroud: Tempus Publishing

Fox, S; 2004, Struggle for Survival – Governing Britain after the Bomb. [Available online at www.subbrit.org.uk]

http://www.manchestereveningnews.co.uk/news/s/236/236056_raid_on_tunnel_network_sparked_big_terror_alert_.html [ONLINE]

http://www.btplc.com/Thegroup/BTsHistory/History.htm [ONLINE]

Chapter 8

Cocroft, W D & Thomas, R J C; 2004, Cold War – Building for Nuclear Confrontation 1946 – 1989. Swindon: English Heritage

http://www.hackgreen.co.uk [ONLINE]

http://www.subbrit.org.uk/rsg/features/war_rooms/index.html [ONLINE]

Chapter 9

Cocroft, W D & Thomas, R J C; 2004, Cold War – Building for Nuclear Confrontation 1946 – 1989. Swindon: English Heritage

http://www.sms-teleport.com/ [ONLINE]
http://www.gvagrimley.co.uk/x2496.xml [ONLINE]

Chapter 10

http://www.ringbell.co.uk/ukwmo/potele.htm [ONLINE]
http://www.portsdown-tunnels.org.uk/cold_war/repeater_station_info.html [ONLINE]

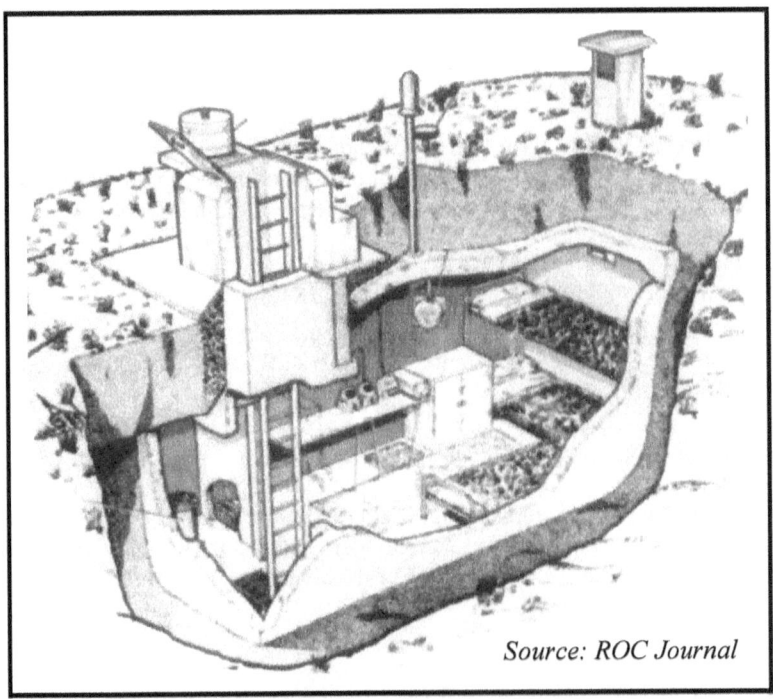

Source: *ROC Journal*

INDEX

A

Acomb (York 20 Group Control), 10, 167, 183-187, 234
Admiralty, 67, 68
Ashmore, Major General Edward Bailey, 68-70
Attack Stages, 15, 36
Auxiliary Fire Service (AFS), 10, 62, 94, 113, 116-126

B

Backbone (Microwave Transmitter Network), 139 - 141, 143
Ballistic Missile Early Warning System (BMEWS), 98, 101
Battle of Britain, 75, 76, 236, 239, 241
Berlin
  Airlift, 20, 21
  Berlin Wall, 19, 22-26
  Blockade, 19, 20
  Marienfelde Refugee Centre, 24, 244
Bomb Power Indicator (BPI), 104, 193, 203, 241
Boyd, Air Commodore Owen Tudor, 71
British Telecom (BT), 137, 138, 141, 226

C

Carrier Control Point, 98, 101, 102
Castro, Fidel Alejandro, 27
Central Electricity Generating Board (CEGB), 133, 223, 226
Chain Home Radar, 75, 76, 85
Chamberlain, Arthur Neville, 73, 74
Checkpoint Charlie, 25, 26
Churchill, Winston Spencer, 13, 18, 74
Civil Defence Corps (CDC), 11, 14, 52, 62, 94, 112-124, 144, 156
Clay, General Lucius Dubignon, 25, 26

Cold War, 7-11, 18, 30, 37, 57, 89, 110, 118, 144, 196, 218, 230, 234, 236, 237, 239, 240, 242-245
  Attack Stages, 15, 36
  Chain of Command / Control Chain, 39
  Nuclear Context, 11-15
  Nuclear Tensions, 19
  Start of ..., 13
  Time Period, 13
Cuban Missile Crisis, 19, 27-29, 43

D

D-Day Landings, 76-77

E

Electro-Magnetic Pulse (EMP), 33, 133, 138
Embry, Air Marshall Sir Basil, 84
Energy Provision, 132-133
Essential Service Route (ESR), 129

F

Fire Service (Brigade), 124, 125, 129
  Auxiliary Fire Service, 10, 62, 94, 113, 116-126
Fiskerton (Lincoln 15 Group Control), 177-182, 236
Fixed Survey Meter (FSM), 193, 199, 200, 204
Friedrichstrasse Border Crossing Point,
  see Checkpoint Charlie
Fylingdales, 98

G

General Post Office (GPO), 78, 136-141, 168, 226
German Democratic Republic, 22, 23
German Federal Republic, 22

Germany: East
  see German Democratic Republic
Germany: West
  see German Federal Republic
Gorbachev, Mikhail Sergeyevich, 13
Gravelines, 65
Green Goddess, 118-120, 125
Ground Zero Indicator (GZI), 182, 194, 197, 241
Grove House (Leeds 8 Group Control), 78, 89, 169, 170

H

Hiroshima, 12, 17, 18

I

Industrial Civil Defence Service (ICDS), 123
Iron Curtain, 13, 239

J

K

Kennedy, John F., 25-28
KGB, 26
Khrushchev, Nikita Sergeyevich, 23, 26-28
Knavesmire (York 9/10 Group Control), 167, 183

L

Lawford Heath (Coventry 8 Group Control), 55, 57, 169-174
London Air Defence Area (L.A.D.A), 68, 69
Los Alamos Range, 17

M

Mallory, Air Chief Marshall Trafford Leigh, 77

Masterman, Air Commodore Edward Alexander Dimsdale, 70
Metropolitan Observation Service, 67
Micklethwait,
  see Post Instrument
Microwave Transmitter Network
  see Backbone
Mobile Columns,
  Auxiliary Fire Service, 120, 121
  Civil Defence Corps, 116
  Fire Service (Brigade), 125
  Police, 129
Mobile Defence Corps, 116
Monitoring Post, 7, 11, 85-88, 92-95, 98, 102, 107, 175, 191-217
Munich Agreement, 74
Mutually Assured Destruction (MAD), 12

N

Nagasaki, 17
Nuclear Attack, 235, 244
Nuclear Burst
  Air, 33
  Ground, 32
  Water / Sea, 33
Nuclear Half-Life, 35
Nuclear Reporting Cell (NRC), 11, 98, 107-109
Nuclear, Biological and Chemical Cell (NBCC),
  see Nuclear Reporting Cell

O

Operation Overlord, 77
Operation Sealion, 75
Operations Room, 83, 84
Orlit (Overground Monitoring Posts), 86-88

P

Police Force, 74, 129
  Cold War, 98, 126-130
  Special Constables, 130
  World War 2, 75, 83

Post Instrument, 80, 81, 86
Potsdam Conference, 24
Primary War Headquarters (PWHQ), 98, 101
Protect and Survive, 35

Q

R

Radiation, 32, 33, 114
Regional Government Headquarters (RGHQ), 55-58, 127, 149-153, 169
Regional Seats of Government (RSG), 12, 38, 43-49, 55, 127, 147, 149
Regional War Rooms (RWR), 38, 40-42, 127, 144
Rotor Plan, 85, 89, 152
(Royal) Observer Corps (ROC), 1, 3, 8, 10, 14, 144, 147, 152, 166-178, 181, 184-188, 191, 192, 195, 196, 199, 200, 202, 203, 206, 210, 211, 216, 234, 238, 240, 242,
  AWDREY, 104-106, 165, 236
  Battle of Britain, 75, 76, 236, 239, 241
  Formation, 71
  Groups/ Sectors, 56, 58
  History, 63-109
  L.A.D.A, 68, 69
  Nuclear, 9, 11, 17, 19, 34, 35, 37, 84, 94, 98, 107, 109, 132, 160, 161, 179, 180, 235, 243-245
  Observation Posts, 80
  Operations Room, 83-84
  Overground Monitoring Posts (Orlit), 85-88

  Seaborne, 76-78
  UKWMO, 11, 91, 93, 102

  Underground Monitoring Post, 93, 193, 194
  World War 1, 67, 69, 73
  World War 2, 7, 74

S

Seaborne, 76-78
Sozialistische Einheitspartei Deutschlands (SED), 23
Spanish Armada, 8, 65-66
Spies for Peace, 44
Stalin, Joseph Vissarionovich, 18, 19, 74
Sub-Regional Control (SRC), 37, 38, 47-49, 127, 149, 150
Sub-Regional Headquarters (SRHQ), 52-55, 125, 127, 144, 149, 152- 154

T

U

United Kingdom Regional Air Operations Centre (UKRAOC), See Primary War Headquarters,
United Kingdom Warning and Monitoring Organisation (UKWMO), 11, 55, 91-93, 95, 97, 102, 107, 166

V, W, X

Y

Yeadon (Leeds 18 Group Control), 175-176
Yorkshire Water Authority, 134, 136, 222

Z

Zeppelin, 67, 68

 **SOUTH YORKSHIRE ROYAL OBSERVER CORPS MUSEUM**

www.ingramcontent.com/pod-product-compliance
Lightning Source LLC
Chambersburg PA
CBHW020353170426
43200CB00005B/153